Metropolitics: A Study of Political Culture

Metropolitics:

John Wiley and Sons, Inc.

New York • London • Sydney

A Study of Political Culture

Scott Greer,

Center for Metropolitan Studies
Northwestern University

(*With the advice and assistance of*
Norton E. Long, *Northwestern University*)

Library of Congress Catalog Card Number: 63-22206
Printed in the United States of America

Foreword

All over the United States the pattern of settlement has been changing until what was an already overwhelmingly urban country bids fair to become an overwhelmingly metropolitan one. The changed and changing pattern of settlement has brought the future structure of local government onto the civic agenda. This is no new thing. As far back as the twenties scholars and "municipal leaguers" were concerned with the metropolitan problem. However, the ever-widening ownership of the automobile, and the consequent revolution in transportation technology and the phenomenal increase in incomes, with the near universalization of the child-centered, middle-class suburban ideal have placed ever-increasing pressure on the capacity of the existing pattern of local governments in metropolitan areas to provide in quantity and quality the civic goods demanded.

The varied dissatisfactions with the local governmental status quo have triggered and will continue to trigger a social search process whose end is the restructuring of local government to meet the effective demands of the citizenry within the emerging constraints of the new patterns of settlement. For the most part the "metropolitan problem" has been treated in the rationalistic terms of utopian civic architecture. It has been a political art form designed to please a narrow circle of the intellectuals of local government. Such reality as it has made contact with has been more that of the sewer and highway engineer than that of the politician or the sociologist. Such conceptions of the political process as have gone into the rationalist artifacts have been largely based on the political folklore of what Merriam called the "prudentes" or the merest conjecture.

The present little volume provides some precious, because woefully scarce, bits of data on the process of governmental change in three metropolitan areas. It recounts the roles of the academics of the study group who provide the documentation, diagnosis, and remedy for the civic ills, the oddly assorted band of agitators who are attracted positively or negatively to exploiting the proposals and the process, the civic notables who provide the means and the testimonial advertising, the press and the other media, and the largely unexplored worlds of the voters as they react to or ignore the stimuli filtered to them. From fragmentary but tangible evidence, Professor Greer sketches out the roles and relationships of a varied set of social and institutional actors who are activated by the threats and promises held forth by the opportunity and even the necessity of social change implicit in the metropolitan problem. The author sketches the common political culture, the political technology, which conditions their perception of the reality to be managed and the available means for its management, and also provides some of the institutional "given" that bounds the action. Professor Greer points to the "morality plays," the preprogrammed responses which provide the voters with their folk wisdom of how to judge what is presented to them. He shows the ambiguity of the performance concocted by the study group and its necessity in view of their constraints. Most importantly he shows what is so frequently neglected by the architects of civic change, the massive power of resistance of the going political system which would be neither going nor a system if it did not have these homeostatic powers.

This book will give little comfort to the power elite school or to the believers in the Oxford Debating Union national democratic voter model. A combination of these two models seems to have inspired the protagonists of change in St. Louis. On the one hand the process of political change is treated as an illness to be diagnosed and prescribed for by politico-medical experts, on the other it is a kind of prestige consumption to be sold through testimonial advertising. This dictates the adman approach, expert and civic notable testimonial mediated to the public through a massive press, radio, and television campaign. The National Oxford Union model is realized in the omnipresent debater and the norm of equal time.

Both of these models get cold comfort from the text. There may however be too pessimistic an appraisal of the appearance of voter incompetence and inattention. Another interpretation can well be that the performance and its lack of vital significance deserved both audience and audience reaction. The record warrants the conclusion that few were deeply serious and these for reasons more personal than public. The record also shows that despite the overwhelming defeat of the District Plan in St. Louis the public at large evinces a continuing receptivity to political change. One may confidently predict the issue will continue to be agitated. Success has and will occur elsewhere. Metropolitan governments of sorts will lose their strangeness and voters will imitate what seems to be working for their civic neighbors.

The present work approaches the phenomena of politics from the point of view of a study in the working of a political culture and the working within the culture of a process of natural selection. Political society like life itself works through "a process of blind variation and selective retention." The results in life are frequently awe inspiring in the elegance of their adaptation. However with the miniscule number of institutional actors in a crowded planet the imposing process of natural selection may be more perilous than we can afford.

NORTON E. LONG

September, 1963

Acknowledgments

As in all studies of society in action, my first debt is to my informants—the scores of political actors and the hundreds of voters I interviewed. Their patience never fails to amaze me.

I also owe a large debt to the various scholars and observers in the three metropolitan areas. Without their help I could not have covered such a broad canvas, even with the thin pigment finally used. I wish to thank Professor Henry Schmandt (now of the University of Wisconsin, Milwaukee), Professors Thomas H. Eliot, Carl McCandless, and David Carpenter of Washington University in St. Louis, and Professor Paul Steinbicker of St. Louis University; Professor Matthew Holden, Jr., now of the University of Pittsburgh; Professor James A. Norton of The Cleveland Foundation, and Mr. Estal Sparlin, of Cleveland, Ohio; Professors Edward Sofen, Thomas Wood, and Ross Beiler, of the University of Miami, for their generous and patient consultation as well as access to unpublished data.

I owe a large debt to the Public Affairs Program of the Ford Foundation. Not only did it support this project, but its support was crucial for the various earlier studies upon which I have relied heavily.

Finally, I wish to thank the field supervisors, Salle Boggs, Dorothy Rosen, and Gilbert James, for their honest and steadfast performance in a difficult job. Mrs. Carola Minar, as research assistant and secretary, has been of inestimable assistance.

Contents

1

Introduction: Morality Plays

of American Civic Life

This study is basically an effort to understand the metropolity in urban America. It focuses on movements aimed at achieving overall metropolitan government in the Miami, Cleveland, and St. Louis metropolitan areas. These are efforts to make revolutions, bloodless to be sure, but far from pacific and rational. Each plan proposes a radical change in the division of power, rewards, and labor in the governance of the metropolis. Each proposes basic changes in the structure of control and in the process by which controllers are recruited. They are minor in the sense that they are proposed within the broad framework of constitutional, democratic, local government. (Each of them assumes a referendum.) Furthermore, they are minor insofar as they are local and segmental, referring only to a part of a local polity, which is, in turn, extremely dependent on the state and federal government levels.

Some people, however, take them very seriously indeed and have elaborate arguments supporting their involvement as well as the particular positions they take upon the issues. We wish, first, to look at these arguments in terms of certain broad norms of government, understandable to a wide array of political actors in the society. We have called these complexes "morality plays," for they are typically dramatic in tone, self-contained in aims, and archetypal in form; they represent vocabularies with which men may converse about common interests or disputes.

The Common Political Culture and Social Action

We emphasize morality plays because they represent an aspect of the common political culture. That is, they represent common definitions of fact and common norms (or rules concerning what ought to be) which are current in the society. Their commonality is their most basic aspect; like threads upon which many kinds of beads may be strung, they allow the coordination of action among diverse persons who play a wide variety of roles in everyday life.

These morality plays provide common definitions of what is, what should be, and how the first may approximate the second. They are crucial for social action; they allow the isolated observer a ready-made framework within which to cast his judgment. Then too, since they are given by official sources (experts, political scientists, and political leaders), they have a presumptive legitimacy. Their wide diffusion through the population and their legitimacy together allow a wide array of people to act as critics of government. The democratization implicit in our political norms, the notion that each man has not only a right but a *duty* to make up his own mind about the substance and form of politics, encourages many citizens, with little trained competence in governmental affairs, to act as kibitzers on the game of politics and government. These judgments are framed by the moralities.

This common political culture is important in another sense. It allows *communication*. Through a common ideological framework, a common vocabulary of norms, the individual's position may be validated by the approval of others. At the same time the culture allows him to influence them. From interaction and influence emerges the possibility of coordination: scattered individuals may be welded into working groups capable of generating social action with possible effects on the broadest arenas. We have seen moralities generate a widespread response which, resulting in coordination around leaders, produced such emergents as the White Citizen's Councils, the John Birch Society, SANE, and the "sit in" movement. In each case direction depends upon a selection from the common culture, reordered for the use of the cadres. The movements for Metro have a similar basis in the common culture.

Finally, because of the wide distribution of power through the vote, the common political culture is crucial in attaining political ends. Though the ideology of the leadership cadres may not be the same as that of the voters, it must be translated into terms that will move them in the desired direction. When the political aim is one which refers, not to candidates and parties, but to the entire constitutional structure, as in these metropolitan government movements, this requirement is crucial. Elections represent a *direct* appeal to the common political culture of the voters. Referenda are so far outside the usual ambit of the electoral machinery that ordinary party goals and tactics have a doubtful relationship to them, if, indeed, any at all is adduced.[1] In short, the workings of democratic elections *without the party system* are clearly visible during such campaigns.

The common culture also has specific limiting effects. Because it focuses on certain aspects of things as they are, because it delineates certain ideal goals out of all those possible, it produces a kind of "tunnel vision." The morality plays of American civic life, for example, seldom transcend the formally governmental. Their emphasis is, again and again, upon the structure of government: the integration of different municipalities, the structural change of county governments, improved public personnel policies, and so forth. Rarely do we see a morality play that attempts to unite the enormous engines of private corporate enterprise (and *their* policies) to those of the public enterprise. Urban renewal is such a play. In short, the common culture of metropolitan reform, the morality plays that allow the actors to organize and speak to the citizens, can be seen as a set of blinders. They reveal certain aspects of the metropolitan area at the cost of suppressing many others.

We have noted and wish to emphasize the historical continuity of the common political culture. The inherited morality plays of American

---

[1] This point will be considered at length in Chapter 4.

civic life may be seen as a conservative tradition of radical reform, conservative in the procedures used in change but radical in the consequences expected. In these dramas, innovators struggle to apply new definitions of broad norms to the specific machinations and actions of their local governments. Out of the conflict between their notions of what should be, derived from these sacred rubrics, they criticize what is. Struggling to change the cities, these innovators emphasize the form of the charters—the constitutions of the cities. (As Adrian has remarked of the National Municipal League: "In its 'model' charters and laws, its booklets and pamphlets, it made available to local groups ammunition that included all of the most recently developed reform favorites.")[2] They frequently go to the voters with their innovations, because of the broader norms of the democratic system.

The movement to improve local government in America has typically dealt with administration and representation. It has aimed at the exclusion of ordinary business interests from the motivations of political officials, at the broadening of the electorate so that the public interest may be represented, at the increased coordination and efficiency possible with professionalism and centralization of local government. Urban home rule, the city manager system, the nonpartisan election (or proportional representation), election at large, the "strong executive," have been some of the specific aims of the movement.

To be sure, not all of these formulas are now in favor with all urban reformers. The general approach has permeated downwards, however, through many strata of the opinionated. We may imagine the public for local government to be a pyramid, with the technical innovators at the top, then the congeries of educated, middle-class men of good will (and ladies, particularly those in The League of Women Voters), the lawyers with vested interests in the subject, and finally the interested citizens. In general, change at the peak of the pyramid does not affect the lower echelons for many years. Thus the technical innovators are bound to the inherited vocabulary because of its utility in communicating with their publics.

[2] Charles R. Adrian, *Governing Urban America*. New York: The McGraw-Hill Book Company, 1955, page 60.

In fact, we may use Sumner's simple natural history scheme to clarify the career of items in the common political culture. That which is current always sets limits upon what may be communicated and used to spark social action. From the new models developed by the inventors, we occasionally have an experimental change of form. Authoritative on a temporary basis (a city "tries" the city manager system) but not sacred, the innovation is a technicway.[3] It is communicable and may "reasonably" be defended, but it is not morally weighted. Technicways, as they become part of the assumed order of things, become conventions—decent people accept them. And presumably, through time, hallowed by their association with legitimate power, they eventually become sacred norms, or *mores*. In some places the city manager system seems to be such a norm.

The process of transformation to the sacred is not clearly understood. Certainly the organizational function of the sacred is important: setting up basic rules of action, we gain the sponsorship of all actors who are committed to the existing order. And even though they may not be personally committed, their very interdependence with those who are means they must play their role, carry out their duties, and exercise their rights. Though we do not really understand how conventions become sacrosanct, we can note a major function of the sacred— the *integrative*. Sacred norms, such as universal manhood suffrage, the right of self-determination, and the right to differ evoke commitment from a very broad segment of the total American electorate. As such, they bring together specialized roles in a kind of unity which permits continuity *even when the details of the government are changed.*

In this sense, sacred norms are probably the greatest asset of government as a continuing and powerful social group. However, between these broadest sacred norms and the office management of the city water works lies an intermediate realm of rules. These may be justified by inclusion under the broader norms, but they may also give way to alternatives equally congruent with the sacred. Such instrumental change may, however, have tremendous effects on the operation of the water works. It is at this level that the morality plays of civic life

[3] Cf. Howard Odum, "Notes on the Techniways in Contemporary Sociology," *American Sociological Review*, Volume II, pp. 336–396.

flourish. Sharp and dramatic conflict is possible between different ways of interpreting the overriding norms.

Images of the City and Themes of Reform

Anselm Strauss has recently documented the ideological resistance of Americans to their urbanization. He shows us clearly the resistance of many kinds of people to the living conditions of a great city.[4] Americans have not easily accepted the concentration of poverty and blight typical of the center city as their ecological home. The "city beautiful" movement of the past, the urban renewal program today, indicate support for a movement to transform the earthly city into the Heavenly City. Equally long-standing and just as impressive has been the struggle to reform the politics of the central city—to take government away from those who regard it as a business, a hunting license for a peculiar kind of game, and turn it into a process as responsible as our idealized memory of the New England townships, as efficient as our stereotypes of the corporate headquarters.[5]

The key arena has been government. The earlier battles for civic reform concentrated on the problems of the central city, for the city's boundaries included reformers and reformees, just as its powers were the key powers for corruption, achievement, change, or stasis. However, the governmental boundaries have shifted greatly with the continuous growth of the city and the outward move of the middle class. Those who care about urban reform are usually suburban in their residence. Robert Wood has noted the congruence of the socially homogeneous, small-scale suburban community with the dream of the "republic in minature." [6] Though Americans have, willy-nilly, become a preponderantly urban people, they have refused to accept an image of the megalopolis as their true home. Instead, they have endeavored to transform the conditions of the great city into "garden towns"—and

[4] Anselm Strauss, *Images of the American City*. Glencoe: The Free Press, 1961.
[5] Adrian, *op. cit.*
[6] Robert C. Wood, *Suburbia, Its People and Their Politics*. Boston: Houghton-Mifflin, 1959.

have, in the suburbs, come close to achieving their aims. The American middle class, in trying to make itself at home in the urban area, has solved many problems by developing suburban neighborhoods separated from the central city by governmental walls.

But other problems have been created in the process. We need not review the consequences of the suburban *begira* for the polity of the urban area as a whole; they have been discussed many times by knowledgeable observers.[7] Let us say in summary that the consequence of governmental proliferation at the municipal level has been to aggravate problems of providing public services, determining equity, and planning for the future. Furthermore, the proliferation of municipalities has prevented development of a polity that might face these problems in any systematic or effective way. These considerations are at the roots of what has been called, in a phrase, "the metropolitan problem." Middle-class persons who were usually those most concerned with governmental reform in the older city solved their personal problems by removing to suburbia. In the process they were also achieving the political dismemberment of the social city. The ghosts of old pieties return to haunt some consciences in suburbia.

The Morality Plays

These ghosts all speak for an image of the city as a unity. And indeed, there is a plausibility in the notion that our contemporary metropolitan areas, despite their hundreds of governments, are still unitary. They represent one local labor market, one housing market, one transport and communication system: they are interdependent in many ways. But in one major way they are different from the city of the past: their governmental boundaries do not include all of the interdependent, problem-generating population. Thus the morality plays that defined the civic problems of the past are still usable: they are simply shifted to a larger stage—the sprawling urban complex which crosses political boundaries of many cities and counties. But now a first condition for

[7] For a recent example see *Exploring the Metropolitan Community*, John Bollens (Editor). Berkeley and Los Angeles: University of California Press, 1961.

resolving the older conflicts in old ways becomes the integration of local government. Seen not as an end in itself, but as a means to older ends, metropolitan government comes to represent a "one best way" to solve many traditional urban problems.

Definitions of these traditional urban problems may be usefully grouped around three kinds of morality plays. Each is as old as urban reform and as American as apple pie. The first is the Purification Ritual, or "Throw the rascals out!" The second might be called the drama of "Capitalist Realism," in which rational men strive to modernize "horse-and-buggy" government. The third is that of fertility and the future: "Progress or Decay! Our City Must Choose!" Each of these plays has a basic cast—heroes, villains, and innocent bystanders. Each has an end in view and a demon in view. Each script assumes the sacrosanctness of the reform and the efficacy of the means to achieve it: all imply that political validation is the one key for opening the way to the Heavenly City.

Purification Rites. In his study of the history of British town planning, William Ashworth attributes public concern for slum clearance, civic beautification, and planning to one major source: middle-class anxiety over disease and crime in the slums.[8] A great deal of the American middle class's concern for local government has been connected with anxieties aroused by evils that threaten their person and pocketbook: the corruption of political office holders, the judges who "sell their eyes," the working relationship between police and criminals known as "the fix."

A typical morality play of Purification begins with indictment of the villains, politicians who have used politics as a business. *The Shame of the Cities* was written by Lincoln Steffens in 1904, but in the late 1950's a national magazine devoted an issue to "The Shame of New York"; the villains remain the same: party politicians, elected officials, policemen, judges. The heroes are typically reform candidates (or officials) playing the role of "Mr. District Attorney." The demon in view is the

[8] William Ashworth, *The Genesis of Modern British Town Planning*. London: Routledge and Kegan Paul, 1954.

threat that "the gangsters will take over the city," that public morality will collapse, that safety of person and property will go by the board. The end in view is the elimination of the corrupt from public office— "surgery"—and their replacement with the upright. These themes recur *ad infinitum* in American civic dramatics. Through time, the major change has been the belief that the political system as a whole is evil, and thus we have the efforts to invent a bureaucracy which will be self-correcting and which will eliminate the corrupt, even as it rewards the just.

Capitalist Realism. The effort to create a self-correcting system is closely allied to the effort to modernize local government. Here the civic demons appear as statistics. The statistics show waste and inefficiency. They show overlapping jurisdictions, confusion of responsibility, and lack of responsibility. They show incompetent men in important offices, competent men bypassed in the decision-making process. The drama has its roots in the speed of change in American society at large, contrasted with the slow pace of governmental change. It is a theme from Dickens or Galsworthy: government remains in chancery, while great problems wait outside the courtroom.

The villains are those who oppose progress, for whatever reason. Their commitment to the *status quo* gives rise to various imputations of dishonesty, malfeasance, or simple stupidity. And the heroes are technicians who are experts in government, businessmen who want to see government run at least as well as the business corporation. From the early efforts to get rid of bicameral legislatures in the cities to the most recent efforts to introduce performance budgets and "scientific personnel management," the drama has been that of mechanical revision, resisted tooth and nail by those who benefit from the *status quo.* It is the attack of the twentieth century on ox-cart government.

The beast in view is the possibility of astronomical costs for little gain, increasingly inadequate services, or breakdowns in such important jobs as police protection and sewerage. The increasing tax bill and the declining service payoff are the bogeys. The aim seems to be to "take garbage collection out of politics" and to turn government into the large-scale public business it should be. Triumph is the achievement of rationality: a perfected bureaucracy operated by professionally trained managers and judged as a business concern.

Fertility and the Future. There is a civic patriotism as old as the planting of new cities, a commitment to hallowed ground. In America, where cities sprang up from the prairie and proliferated with the spread of the railroad, every crossroad hamlet has aspired to be the "Chicago of Wyoming," the "Metropolis of the Permian basin." The great plains and the deserts are littered with the bones of would-be metropolitan communities.[9]

Such cities were efforts to get rich quick. Their pioneers were entrepreneurs, and their slogan was "Boost, don't knock!" Their fortunes were measured by the increase in population, carloadings, and bank accounts. New building, any new building, was a sign of prosperity for all. This civic drama has always assumed a biological metaphor with growth as the good and decay as the horrible alternative. And growth is a result of massing what exists so that more may exist in the future. (Witness the outcry in Chicago when the Bureau of the Census decided to treat the Indiana portion of that metropolitan area as a separate unit.) "Boosterism" reflects a synthesis of the economic man's wish to improve his market and the civic patriot's identification with his city as home.

The heroes of such a drama are the "forward-looking, aggressive civic leaders," who want to make this city "the greatest center of paper-box manufacturing in the country." They act by organizing, building, advertising, allowing more room for growth (and hence, presumably, room at the top). The villains are those who have an unassailable position in the *status quo,* who resist change. Like the politician who prefers to lose an election rather than to lose control of his party, they would rather see the city remain stable. Every large city has its mythology about the "five families who own this town and don't want to see it change." But the beast in view is the spectacle of the town declining, losing ground in national rank orders. The fear is that of a shrinking market and a backward, physically unpleasant scene for living.

[9] For a fascinating local history of such a would-be city see Wallace Stegner's *Wolf Willow.*

Morality Plays and the Movement for "Metro"

Such are three of the more salient morality plays of our civic life. They are widely understood by the kind of actors who may become leaders in reform: presumably they are also communicable to the voters. Each of them focuses attention and judgment on certain aspects of the local political-governmental scene and excludes other aspects.

(1) The Purification Rite rests on the private morality of the American middle class. It emphasizes the application of universalistic norms, of general moral rules that apply to all, in the day-to-day actions of officials. Historically, it has focused rather straitly on elected officials in the *political parties* and, more narrowly, on the government of the *central city*. The reasons seem fairly clear: the central city is the big budget and payroll of the metropolis, it is usually partisan in its politics, and its politics are nearly always dominated by the party. Its government has leverage on many private enterprises. The morality of purification tends to ignore suburbia, where government is small-scale, parties hardly operate, and few persons gain much financially from politics. The assumption is that small municipalities, controlled by "friends and neighbors," (assumed to be middle-class also) perform honestly and legally. In point of fact, nobody knows whether this is true or not. The negotiations for bond issues, the decisions on land use, the issuance of licenses are all obvious possibilities for lucrative "deals" even in rather small municipalities. Despite an occasional note in a central city paper, however, such suburban enclaves are not usually the scene of the Purification Ritual.[10]

---

[10] Cf. *The St. Louis Post Dispatch*, editorial, Tuesday, November 10, 1959. Referring to the government of the suburban county, the editorialist writes: "Each of the offices in which deficiencies were found is headed by an elected official, as indeed are all the major administrative agencies in the court-house. These officials need no qualifications to file for office and once elected, take orders from nobody. Each is an independent political boss, tenderly solicitous for the patronage employees who represent the means to re-election." Such comments apply equally well to many suburban municipalities, but they simply do not "get the billing," perhaps because of the economies of newspaper investigation and reporting.

(2) "Capitalist realism" rests on American faith in efficiency and business. It tends to emphasize the efficiency of government as a business enterprise. The whole organization of government is seen as subordinate to its provision of goods and services, from police protection to garbage removal. In highlighting the economic output, however, the morality tends to emphasize economies; the typical drama has been one aimed at "getting rid of the deadwood," "ending featherbedding," "increasing efficiency." The analogue to the marketplace is the citizen demanding quality goods at the cheapest price.

Such an approach tends to elide two important aspects of the public enterprise. First, the heads of government are not simply entrepreneurs operating with public capital: they are also, and preeminently, *representatives* of the citizens in their relations with government. Second, the morality play tends to assume a stable rather than an expanding market for governmental goods and services. What citizens *might* want from government, if they had a real array of choices, is in the nature of things unknown. Thus the morality of capitalist realism is inherently anti-political and tends to be conservative in its aims.

(3) The Fertility Ritual rests on belief in an automatic progress for all Americans (and therefore American cities), tempered with awareness of the competition for living space among both citizens and cities. It is assumed that a city can grow indefinitely, if its leaders only understand the techniques; if they fail, other cities will take its place in the sun. Sheer quantitative growth has historically been accompanied by astronomical increases in some kinds of problems; it has entailed the in-migration of foreigners, a pool of unskilled and uneducated labor, the continuation of housing shortages, and looseness of political morality. But the emphasis on growth *per se* leaves little room for concern with its side effects.

Thus the fertility rituals have not usually drawn attention to the quality of life in the city. Average income, for example, might be a better indicator of improving quality than simple population increase. (Some of the most rapidly growing cities on earth, in Asia, Africa, and Latin America, are also the poorest). But the morality of growth assumes an automatic increase in amenities with the simple increase in population, carloadings, and bank accounts. The provision and improvement of such services as museums, symphonies, libraries, schools, parks, and playgrounds, instead of being a basic focus, is incidental to the fertility ritual. In fact, these services can be justified (within the conventional drama) only as possible stimuli to further economic growth. In the same way, comprehensive land-use planning is seen, not as providing goods often substitutable for the results of sheer growth, but as *incentives for growth*. The fertility drama rests upon an anxiety suspiciously similar to that of the real estate broker when business is slow.

The "Metropolitan Mix" of Themes

These morality plays each influenced the definition of the metropolitan government as it was presented to the citizens in St. Louis, Cleveland, and Miami. The conservative tradition of reform in local affairs set the limits within which the plans were drafted, and within which their salient characteristics were defended.

In these three cities those who drafted the new charters envisaged a federal system in which existing units of government would be preserved. The new metropolitan government was seen as a vehicle to achieve what could not be done with the existing fragmented system. The radical nature of the departure was minimized, for the new plans did not attack *existing* governments so much as the existing "metropolitan system" of government. The morality of Purification was, in general, ignored. Nobody fighting for the plans could exploit the old slogan "Throw the rascals out!" The drafters of the plans seemed to assume that all were victims of the historical lag between government and the growing urban area.

The reasons for omitting the Purification Ritual have been as follows. First, in St. Louis and Cuyahoga, there was genuine belief in the integrity of existing governments *within their limits*. The long-term effort to tame municipal politics through professional management and civil service had been relatively successful in these cities. In Dade County there had been some extreme dissatisfaction with the government of Miami.[11] The belief in the integrity of existing government combined, in St. Louis and Cleveland, with a desire to neutralize the political parties, since it was thought that they might defeat any charter that threatened their organization and patronage systems. The campaigns deliberately avoided antagonizing the party chieftains. At most the supporters of the plans said "we will give you administration by experts, under elected officials responsible to the voters."

The metropolitan movement is, then, squarely in the tradition of capitalist realism. The organizational merging of the multifarious local governments for areawide services, the emphasis on metropolitan area planning and zoning, the predominance of appointed rather than elected heads for the great bureaucracies, all point to the image of technical efficiency as a goal. The Dade County plan even went so far as to specify an appointed county manager for the metropolitan area, and in both St. Louis and Cuyahoga County the issue of an elected versus an appointed head was the source of ideological conflict from study commission to voter. The vision of a new, bright, freshly painted and efficient government was presented to the voters. As a minor theme, in each area the increased "home rule" which would accrue to the metropolitan county or district was noted. This was most important in Dade County, which had been largely dominated from the state capital in Tallahassee. In St. Louis and Cleveland a large degree of home rule already existed and the theme was not very important in these campaigns.

The Fertility Ritual was a major element in each city. In St. Louis particularly, the consciousness of "decay" and the desire to continue a supposed "renaissance" was a crucial part of the campaign. In Miami, the dependence upon tourism and retirement and the assumed relationship between these economic assets and local services is given credit

[11] "People really believed the hair-raising stories that you heard about the police sitting around with their feet on the tables, reading the scratch sheets with direct wires to the books." (*Interview Protocol* with a major executive in the mass media.) The Kefauver Committee supplied some evidence for such beliefs.

by one observer for almost all of the interest manifested in Metro by the business community and the civic leaders.[12] In one of the major pieces of campaign literature distributed by supporters of the St. Louis District Plan, economic development occupies the center of the stage.

All surveys . . . show that our area is losing out to Kansas City, Chicago, Memphis, Dallas, and other places in attracting wealth-producing industry and commerce . . . By voting for the District Plan, we can start to return to our rightful place—as the major Mid-American district between the Atlantic and the Pacific.[13]

And how was this to be achieved? We quote from the same leaflet:

The District Plan will give us a chance to plan for the entire city-country area—not just one part at a time—so that industry, commerce, and residential developments can be located where they belong without destroying property values. It will set up a means for private and public groups to work together—to plan and assemble industrial parks—away from residential areas—to offer new industry at cost. And by eliminating some of our other problems, such as the traffic mess, we'll have a chance to compete successfully for new business, and thousands of new jobs, which helps *everyone*.[14]

In short, the metropolitan government was a new means to old ends— economic prosperity, a better market for the individual, and a better city for the average resident.

These movements for metropolitan government relied heavily on two of the traditional morality plays of American civic life. Each emphasized the need to modernize local government through job analysis, coordination, and realignment of boundaries. Each offered improved services to the citizens as a reason for doing so. Each promised improvement in the local economy and, therefore, the value of the city as a place in which to work and to live.

[12] Reinhold P. Wolff, *Miami Metro*. Coral Gables, Florida: Bureau of Business and Economic Research, 1960.
[13] "Some Plain Answers to Questions about the Greater St. Louis City-County District Plan." St. Louis: City-County Partnership Committee, 1959.
[14] *Ibid*.

Plot and Counterplot in the Morality Plays

If the public is accustomed to a given morality in the rhetoric of reform, that morality's absence will be quickly noted. The decision *not* to attack incumbent officials and existing governments for their incompetence and inability weakened the hands of the crusaders. Mounting an offensive which did in fact threaten many alignments and jobs (each plan took important powers away from municipal officials, and the Cuyahoga plan even dispensed with Civil Service safeguards), the plans provoked hostility from key members of the establishment without providing any ammunition to return their fire.

The head of a major department in the city of Cleveland gleefully related the advantage he had in fighting against the Cuyahoga County Charter.

> I'd say to them, "Say—what's wrong with the present situation? You got a good government. What's wrong? Show me?" I'd get right down to specifics—"what's been done wrong?"

Bypassing the elected representatives of the *status quo* thus pulled a key member out of the morality plays' structure. It left the elected officials blameless and free to attack the new plan from the rostrum of public office. (This made logical sense, however, if it was only the lack of a *single* system that was at fault.) As we shall see, this decision had important consequences for the campaigns in St. Louis and Cleveland.

The elimination of the Purification Ritual also affected the plausibility of the efficiency engineering approach. The decision to leave all municipalities in existence made the plans extremely vulnerable to those who felt that the existence of a multitude of governments was a handicap in attaining good governance. The first reason given by Mayor Tucker in his first speech opposing the District Plan hinged on this belief.

> *The proposed metropolitan District Plan does not eliminate one existing area government—with the exception of its absorption of the metropolitan sewer district.*

The 99 country municipalities, the 21 fire districts, the separate City and County, and all the rest remain. Each of them is unimpaired in its present tax-levying authority.[15]

In St. Louis, the District Plan suffered from this further debility—it really added an additional government to the ones in existence. Though the other two plans escaped this through using existing county governments as bases for the metropolitan district, each was vulnerable to the attacks of purists who wished to see radical surgery on the governmental proliferation in the area.

The morality of "capitalist realism" suffered also from the tendency of the pro-Metro leaders to tell the truth. Instead of promising savings through increased efficiency, many of them tended to emphasize the *increase in services* possible through a Metro government. Again, this was less true of Dade County. There the leaders of the revolution were prone to hold out the carrot of lower taxes (though privately they believed Metro could only attack the areawide service problems through increased taxation). In St. Louis, the protagonists tried to counter the "higher taxes" argument by showing that the plan would increase the fertility of the region and therefore its tax yield at existing rates.

The Fertility Ritual was not in basic conflict with the efficiency engineering and did not suffer from the absence of the Purificatory Rites. In did suffer, however, from its abstract and novel nature. While citizens are accustomed to hortatory slogans to "buy local," to "boost St. Louis," and the like, they are not used to the rather intricate argument supporting metropolitan government as a source of future fertility. First, the argument moves from unknown to unknown—from land-use planning to plant location—and finally to greater local prosperity, lower taxes, and better services. Second, and perhaps more important, the possibility of land-use planning depends on the *time element*. Comprehensive land-use planning has never been popular or popularly understood, for it requires a knowledge of the effects of present political acts upon consequences many years in the future. This is the dilemma of those who see most present problems as produced by past planning

[15] Mayor Raymond F. Tucker, St. Louis: for release 7:00 p.m. Saturday, October 3, 1959.

failures: to change present planning requires that they use, as evidence, the very complex chain of events from lack of past planning to the contretemps of today. Metropolitan government, in the context of the Fertility Rites, presents a complex *answer* to people who have never understood the *questions*—much less asked them.

In summary: the metropolitan morality play leaned heavily on two earlier plots. It omitted the most familiar of all and the one with the greatest "box office" appeal—"throw the rascals out." Omission of this theme greatly weakened the most clearly understood argument that was used—"Get rid of ox-cart government"—for it left the *status quo* standing. While the efficiency engineering approach and the Fertility Ritual were mutually reinforcing, the latter was largely outside the conventional realm of discourse. The chief argument shared by the rebels and the general public was that of mechanical progress aimed at greater service benefits. It was weakened by a "live and let live" philosophy with respect to the existing municipalities. It was strengthened by demand for better services. It used the older drama of boosterism, though many did not understand the plot.

Within this metropolitan morality play the protagonists of reform organized themselves and made sense of their proposal to create a revolution in urban government. They defined their roles as crusaders for a new "one best way" to achieve the Heavenly City. They defined their enemies as the protectors of separatism, in bond to the *status quo* (leaving, however, the "dark man" of professional politics as an ambiguous character). The cadres were developed, the struggle was joined, and eventually the voters were approached, in this vocabulary.

But we are getting ahead of our story. First it is necessary to ask: Who were the radicals, and where did they come from?

2

The Dramatis Personae of

Reform and Resistance

Looking at the kaleidoscope of social relationships presented by the metropolitan world, it is difficult indeed to discern structure. Even though we move through the corridors of an organizational maze—the corporate world of the fortieth floor, the world of state and federal governmental agencies or City Hall—it is still difficult to see more than shifting clues of an order. Though we run head-on into organizational constraint (in traffic, courtroom, or bankruptcy proceeding) we are still puzzled by what has been called "the architecture of the maze." We are certain only of one thing—we do not deal with individuals as single events, but move within an order that controls our relations with others. In this world, "where centaurs walk, half-men, half-reputation," it is frequently the reputation that provides clues to the structure.

Reputation is, in the broadest sense, an estimate of the potency for social action inherent in others. Such estimates are made continually in our everyday life: when they become socially current they constitute one of the bases for order in society. However, the investigator of the social order also uses them as a tool. He estimates potency for social action by *position*, by place within an organized group or within a reputationally stratified social world. The singular events of social interaction are connected by the invisible bonds of organization; where such bonds endure through time in a predictable pattern, we deal with an effective constraint on individual behavior. Shop, factory, corporation; precinct club, or city agency; city council or chamber of commerce— such organizations are the constituent parts of the maze.

These constituent organizations are not, however, arranged in any simple "table of organization," nor do they coincide in their boundaries. They are, instead, an *ecology of orders,* from household to corporation and municipality. They order the sprawling metropolitan settlement and its population in a loose but minimally integrated fashion. Rarely are such organizations coterminous with a contemporary metropolis: they are partial in membership—geographically and socially exclusive. And usually, an organizational network includes any given part of a population in a structure spread much wider than the metropolitan area. Thus the metropolitan community is not, in social fact, a single organization in any sense.

When, therefore, we turn to consider the actors who become involved in the enterprise of metropolitan reform, we look to an organizational topography. These masses of moving actors are related in larger and smaller *systems,* having greater or less control over their members as well as over the conditions of existence for outsiders. It is from position in organizations that individuals derive the opportunity and resources to influence collective enterprises: organizational and reputational position are the bases for social action. From what organizational stronghold, then, does a movement for metropolitan integration issue? Who provides the logistic necessities and decides the strategy of campaign? Where does opposition arise and how is it supported? These are important questions. They may be rephrased: what segments of the organizational structure of a metropolitan congeries are willing to integrate the sprawl in an imaginary and unprecedented government?

Where Do They Come From?

To make a revolution is hard, as Machiavelli and others have noted. Those who will lose usually see their interest much more clearly than those who will gain. To make the metropolitan revolution is as hard as most such assignments. This is especially true when the objective is to make the change from below through referendum and not from above by *diktat* (as was done in New York and Toronto). We need only look at the history of failure over the past forty years or more, in dozens of American metropolitan areas, to appreciate the difficulty. Though St. Louis was separated from the then rural county and integrated in 1876, and New York consolidated in 1898, the recent history of metropolitan efforts in large cities is generally one of failure. (One significant exception is Miami, of which more later). Of metropolitan revolutionaries one may say, with literal truth, "They went forth to battle but they always fell." How, then, is it possible to account for this recurrent though bootless effort?

Perhaps the simplest and most useful way of answering the question is to formulate another. In whose interest is a campaign for metropolitan government valuable? This differs from the related question: In whose interest is the *accomplishment* of such a government valuable? Some persons seem primarily interested in the crusade, whether or not Jerusalem is sighted, while others have genuine stakes in getting there. These questions can be answered through some general principles of engagement. First, it is *occupationally* useful for some persons to launch and/or win such a campaign. Second, it is *reputationally* useful for others. Utility does not imply cynicism: use may be instrumental or terminal. Let us say there is a probability of achieving valued ends, directly or indirectly, for some persons, through the medium of a metropolitan government movement. They are a far from random sample of the metropolitan population.

Occupational utility is derived from position in the organizational topography of the metropolis. There are, first, the free professionals whose vocation is contingent upon the local governmental and political system. Lawyers, public relations people, and the like periodically or regularly swim in the streams of political gossip, patronage, and career. They are "experts" whose expertise makes them eligible for such activity as a reform crusade. There are also the political, economic, and voluntary organizational leaders and professionals. For them, participation in the campaign may be due to (1) their role in an organized group and the duties and rights intrinsic to that role (one may be the "community relations officer" of a major firm) or (2) the perceived interests of the organization as a whole in the outcome of the campaign (the location of an expressway matters to a department store).

Such actors might be termed the "Hessians" of local governmental activity. Quite different are those who move in terms of a vague set of role expectations based on general preeminence or presumed expertise —the civic notables and the men of good will. These might be considered to work for community welfare, through a norm of "noblesse oblige." They are men of civic reputation, whether for leadership stature, experience, or both. They are sometimes self-selected, though on occasions it is clear that they are put "on the spot" and forced to take a stand, willy-nilly. As noted earlier, it is incorrect to assume that such persons act in a "disinterested" manner. The maintenance and increase of reputation and the fulfilling of role obligations based on it are positive goods, made tangible in the responses of others and in their own movement within the vaguely defined stratification system of local repute.

Their Order of Appearance

There are, roughly, four phases in the life history of a metropolitan reform movement. These are (1) initiation, through agitation and study, (2) gaining validation at the top, by harnessing the notables, (3) defining innovation, by drafting the new constitution, and (4) gaining effective validation from the community, through running the campaign. The phases overlap and interlock in terms of personnel, but it is useful to look carefully at the kinds of persons who become involved at each stage. We shall consider the protagonists of change first, for their actions are coterminous with the entire drama.

The Agitators. The rebels who first light the brands of revolt are typically men marginally committed to the existing structure of political affairs. They include professional politicians who are not on friendly terms with the dominant coalition—Republicans in the central city, liberals in the suburbs. Included also are intellectuals who feel they have no access to the polity of the area as a whole. (Indeed, one suspects they support a large-scale metropolitan government in order to have something that *could* transmit their ideas into politics for their community). In St. Louis, the political scientists were a major factor in translating agitation of the Cervantes group for a traffic and transit district into a broad look at the metropolitan area as a whole. A final class of agitators might be termed the "free-floating kibitzers of local government." From Citizens Leagues and Good Government Councils, Bureaus of Research and committees of one kind and another, a snaffle of individuals in every city becomes reputationally involved in governmental reform.

This Coxey's Army then moves the proposal for change towards the study stage. From local sources (interested or disinterested organizations) and (with the support of local civic leaders) from foundations, the agitators raise the money to mount their comprehensive study of government in the locale. This study is typically staffed with persons from outside, experts in metropolitan government. Outside experts, in turn, support the contention that the evolving plan for change is scientific in its origins and nature, free of local interest struggles and unbiased in its results.

The study group, though captained by outside mercenaries, is usually staffed from local resources. Many of these local persons turn out to be intimately associated with the local agitators. Furthermore, the outside captains, being political scientists interested in local government reform, are familiar with the free-floating kibitzer, the dissatisfied liberal, the amateur of local government. Congeniality results, and the agitators become a guerilla army for the campaign of study, a CIA for the study director.

The study organization then operates within a circle of reference groups, which are far from representative of either the power or the people in the metropolis. Indeed, study groups are typically suspended, like Mohammed's coffin, between heaven and earth. Earth is represented by the political facts of life in the metropolis, heaven by the staff's professional community. Under the banner of the "one best way," they conceive of studies as achievements in an art form, whose product, "The Plan," is to be judged against the monumental utopias of the past.

There is, however, a bonus for the study director if his plan is passed. Thus the construction of a Utopia is considerably affected by the question of electability. This must be judged by local evidence. Much of it is filtered through the intelligentsia of government in the *locale,* for another aspect of their utility lies in bridging the gap between the research group and the local notables.

The Chorus of Old Men. The civic notables are important in the early stages of the campaign; their organizational prominence and reputational height lend dignity and legitimacy to the campaign. We have already noted that they are important in validating the issue as worthy of study, and may even arrange support for such studies. Civic notables are typically integrative symbols of the "metropolitan community": this is the form and nature of their reputation. Based in universities, foundations, the churches, the schools, the newspapers, the chamber of commerce, they stand for the welfare of the community at large. Many of them are citizens of large organizations with a long-run stake in the downtown, or in the metropolitan area as a whole.

Thus we find, in every campaign, owners and editors of the mass media. The *Post Dispatch, Miami Herald, Cleveland Press*—each was more than a mirror for events. Leading executives in these firms became supporters of the campaign. Television and radio are also important in providing support. And, because of the involvement of civic notables who are in these businesses, the resources of the enterprise are used (hopefully) to advance the cause. This involves a multitude of hired professionals—news commentators, reporters on the City Hall beat, public relations men. The market value of a crusade, for the mass media, tends to flood the scene with symbol manipulators.

The mass media have an areawide public. They are concerned with areawide issues—both substantively and esthetically. Certain other types of enterprise are areawide in scope; their officers therefore take a broader view than do those who are citizens of central city or of suburb. Among these, the utilities are of major importance: their stake is in the metropolis as a whole and their executives are typically civic notables, drawn into the support of the campaign. The campaign is substantively in line with the long-term interests of the utility industry, while the short-run publicity value attached to identifying with the interests of the area as a whole is seen as good.

Somewhat different are the interests of those committed to the down-town, the older central business district. Such organizations include business with plant commitments downtown, downtown department stores, real estate firms with holdings in the central business district, banks in states disallowing branch banking, and the blue-collar labor unions. They are concerned with preserving the economic position of the central business district in a rapidly suburbanizing metropolis. Thus they may also be realistically in favor of some governmental arrangement that would facilitate the "salvation of the downtown business district." They are committed to the continued vitality of the center, and the rhetoric of "the metropolitan community" may cloak their special interest, while advancing the probability of an areawide change which would aid the center.

The Constitutional Assembly. Here we find the greatest discrepancy among the three cities. The machinery of the State constitutions allows for a wide variety in the selection processes for the Charter Commission. In Cleveland, the Democratic party slate won most of the seats; most of the Commission was selected to represent certain factions and interests in the party at various levels, with maverick Republicans to represent the rest of people in the area. In Dade County the commission was chosen through the legislature and governor, though probably hand-picked by the state senator. It was representative of the various local governments in the area—major Miami suburbs, past office-holders, county officials, local notables, and the like. In St. Louis, a complex and curious system resulted in nominations by circuit judges (with seconds by the city's mayor and the suburban county's supervisor) and one man picked by the governor.

The personnel of the assemblies thus chosen varied considerably. They tended to include, however, men who were either (1) politicians, (2) amateur experts in local government, (3) notables interested in the problem, or (4) representatives of minorities—Negroes, suburbs, labor, and Republicans. Furthermore, most of them were known as "civic leaders," of whatever stature: they were men of good will.

The Campaigners. Those who were campaigning for the new government were persons who, because of occupational or reputational position, had an interest in radical reform. If they were marginal to the process of government—intellectuals, "outs," or helpless minority representatives—their aim was simple: to change the rules and improve their chance for winning. If, however, they were "ins," their concern was to improve a winning game. Thus the cadres who supported reform represented a split in the "political class" brought about by differences in advantage and perquisite, a few persons who saw a means of going from "in" to "inner circle," and a wide array of amateurs. As one protagonist with political experience wryly observed, "We've got all the do-gooders on our side, every damned one of them—even the non-Gibbons Teamsters (whom we managed to lose), and we have the endorsement of the ADA (Americans for Democratic Action) which we've also managed to bury, and some former mayors—Oh, we've got 'em all."

We may divide the campaigners for the reform movement into five categories. These include (1) professionals, (2) economic owners and managers who are civic notables, (3) public officials, (4) party officials not in office, and (5) private organizational officials.

The professionals include underemployed lawyers interested in building up publicity and practice, breaking into politics, or simply keeping busy. Both sides had impressive arrays of forensic talent. Other professionals include the professors in local colleges and universities, whose presumed expertise gave them some weight as speakers and whose reputation conferred upon them the opportunity and duty to demonstrate; journalists, who covered City Hall and took a professional interest in the campaign as a good thing (such journalists range from men with broad learning to inside "dopesters"); public relations officials, who usually get involved on a for hire basis but become committed to *this* campaign in a more than usual way; and finally, those research persons ordinarily concerned with municipal government and civic betterment. Thus, in short, most of the intelligentsia of local public affairs gets involved as protagonist of metropolitan reform.

Economic owners and managers who become involved fall into one of the general "interest involvement" categories stated earlier. In each city, executives from the newspapers, radio, television, and public relations firms, universities, and the like gave at least nominal support. That is, they made statements for consumption through the media. Furthermore, executives from utilities, banking firms, and real estate development concerns were quite prominent in the campaigns. Although most of the economic resources in St. Louis were channeled through the Civic Progress group (which will be discussed later), this was not true in Cleveland. The donors, however, were heavily concentrated among the types of industry cited, plus some aid from massive corporations which confer a *de facto* position of leadership upon anyone who heads them locally.

Public officials, of course, could not avoid entanglement with the issue once it had emerged into the light of day and become the subject for a referendum. However, such public leaders were split on the issue, with the great majority in the central city opposing the new plan of government, whatever it was. There were exceptions: General Evans, the City Manager of Miami, supported change, as did Porter, the County Engineer of Cuyahoga County, while Cervantes, the President of the St. Louis City Board of Aldermen, was the spearhead of the district campaign. There is reason to believe that, in each case, the new form of government seemed likely to improve a winning game for these individuals.

Elected public officials who became involved as protagonists of change in the suburbs included a minority among the city managers, councilmen, mayors, city attorneys, officials in the county government, state legislators, and the like. In general, those most active were, as might be expected, elected officials. One exception to this rule is the great activity of those lawyers who acted as appointed city attorneys for municipalities in the suburbs.

Party officials were split, in central city and in suburbs. Club chairmen, committeemen, aspirants, and past candidates were relatively free to choose as they wished. Many made strong public statements in favor of the reform, but very few used whatever political muscle was available to them as party leaders. In general, the party leaders most active *were* the protagonists of change. These, however, were the "outs," the permanent and temporary minorities, the marginal politicos.

They tended to act, then, not as leaders in the political armies but simply as private citizens who favored reform.

Private voluntary organizational leaders included a wide variety of persons. They had one thing in common: they stood as representatives of some organized interest. In addition, they were mostly newcomers to political action of this kind. As one campaign worker wistfully remarked, "We're not 100 per cent amateurs, but we don't have the contacts that would be desirable." The chambers of commerce, in central city and suburbs, supported the campaigns, as did the League of Women Voters, the churches and church federations, and professional groups such as planners, architects, and those concerned with "welfare" services.

We might draw a line between organizations with specialized interests and those with generalized interests. The latter were most likely to support the campaign with resources and personnel. The more specialized groups, however, tended to remain neutral or to oppose change. Even if they formally endorsed the plan, they acted in such a desultory fashion that one guessed it was not their fight. Here Machiavelli's dictum applies with force: groups organized for corporate protection are extremely sensitive to the damaging consequences of reform—but they have to be shown in detail any profit that might accrue to them through change.

From these five classes of organizational actors, *ad hoc* campaign committees were organized. These committees were nominally representative of the city fathers, the integrative leaders, the notables. In St. Louis, the committee was supported through public endorsement and cash, by Civic Progress. However, the leadership of the Citizens Committee for City-County Partnership, a post of great symbolic significance, did not go to a major figure. Instead, it seems that the notables of the first water shrank from the glory and, after several had declined, turned finally to a political unknown. He was a person with a reputation for good works, a war hero who had sponsored the local "boys town." An unexceptionable young man, he had no history or particular competence in local political affairs; the campaign was his baptism of fire. Both the abnegation of the "Big Mules" and the choice of this man as leader indicate the contingent commitment of big business to the campaign.

One of the important leaders of the protagonists raised the following question:

> What kind of a civic leadership do you have around here when the town's dying and you've got a bunch of young punks—average age 35 or so—running a campaign like this? Where are Clark, Chedayne, Calhoun? James is in his 30's, Cervantes is 38, I'm 33, Chris Donahue's 42. What gives? Those guys in Civic Progress have given us damned near nothing.
>
> Oh, we're strong in the MAC and the Racquet Club. But what kind of help do we get besides their votes? Nothing. We'll carry Portland Place!

In the campaign committees the division of labor tended to elevate professional politicians to the chief of staff position: their presumed expertise and political ties justified such a role. The staff work was performed largely by a mixture of the intelligentsia of local government and the political leaders' lieutenants. The leg work, insofar as it was carried out at all, was assumed by the League of Women Voters and the underemployed young lawyers. The League carried on the house-to-house canvassing, the telephone campaign, the mailing of leaflets, the organizing of *kaffee klatsches* for speakers, and the like. The young lawyers carried the bulk of the speaking engagements. They went on the hustings before captive audiences at meetings of voluntary organizations. They explicated the "plan" drawn up by the Commission. They attempted to translate the general interest argument into the special interests of their audiences.

Like the chairman of their committee, they were professionally and occupationally involved in the city, whether the campaign won or not, and they tended to emphasize integrative and ameliorative symbols. Those who were drawn into these campaigns were preponderantly marginally engaged in the cause, and the campaigns were remarkably civil and courteous. Though the issue split occupational groups, municipal governments, political parties, and even families, it is our judgment that the conflict rarely left permanent scars.

The Hard-Core Resistance

Opponents to the campaign for metropolitan government were slow to show their hand. To be sure, from the early days of the campaign various eccentrics displayed their chauvinism in small arenas. By and large, however, those who were opposed to any metropolitan government and those who ended up in opposition to the specific plan counseled "wait and see." Only after the charters were legally fixed and the referendum campaign began did the true extent of the opposition become clear. And that opposition was directly deducible from a knowledge of the existing structure of government in the metropolitan areas.

In the central cities, the mayors of St. Louis and Cleveland were opposed. For them there was much to lose and little to gain. The department heads of the central city likewise thought in cool business terms: the vast enterprises they managed (port and airport facilities, roads and highways, welfare and hospitals, and on and on) should not be lightly donated to some unknown governmental entity. Central city political actors looked with great suspicion upon the new government. Nor could they easily be persuaded that the new government had plums for them. Cervantes described one of his lieutenants who, when told of the new patronage available, responded: " 'Look Al, it all sounds nice but where is the hooker? Them college professors aren't going to do something for us. Where's the hooker, Al?' Naw, the Wards aren't with us. They don't care. My own people say to me, 'Sure Al, I'll do it for you Al,' but . . .'" (grins) It is likely that many political actors would have preferred to sidestep the issue. This option was frequently closed to them by the pressure of those who were already involved: forced to take a stand, they sometimes gave lukewarm support and sometimes became violent opponents.

The constituent interest groups of the central city were also suspicious of the projected metropolitan government. In both Cleveland and St. Louis, the Negro wards voted almost solidly against reform. They saw the new government as a threat to the existing representation of Negroes in the central city council; indeed, specific office-holders saw their positions in danger of abolition. The entire existing structure, from household to precinct to ward and council, was threatened. The response was well-nigh unanimous.

While labor unions split between those opposed and those paying lip service to the campaign, general strategy was passive resistance. The reasons, again, derive from the destructive consequences the metropolitan government would have for existing political agreements and coalitions. Too many new and unforeseeable elements were to be introduced into what seemed a winning game. Therefore the specialized "political representatives" of labor were, for the most part, from cool to frigid with respect to reform.

In the suburban areas, opposition was widespread and vociferous. The mayors of small suburban municipalities, their councilmen, and their city attorneys constituted the cadres that spoke against the plan and debated with its protagonists. Municipal employees were panicked at the notice that they might lose their job security in a new and unknown government. Small businessmen suspected that, should control of streets and zoning be ceded to a larger government, their own ability to appeal and influence decisions would wither away. They sensed the loss of "community integrity," which was defined as an asset to their business district—and business.

The resulting noise was multiplied manyfold by the space devoted to arguments against metropolitan government in the suburban community press. These newspapers had both a vested interest in the campaign and an interest in its defeat. Furthermore, the spectre of metropolitan government was a useful target for newspapers which can rarely afford a strong and crusading stand. The reason is implicit in their usual *modus vivendi*: strong positions are avoided because they are divisive. Here, however, was a major issue which could be used to integrate the paper with the community, *against* such easy targets as the wicked city politicians, the dying and bankrupt central city, the multitudinous and dangerous strangers who roamed outside the local bailiwick. Furthermore the community newspapers, insofar as the local shopping district and the committed home-owners of the community were their source of revenue and readership, had nothing to gain with the blurring of municipal boundaries. Quite the contrary. The fiction of community autonomy in the suburbs is a powerful legitimizer for the local community press. Thus the little papers were not undistorting mirrors any more than the central city dailies: they were wholeheartedly committed to opposition.

Finally, the net effect of this opposition was to line up the political organizations—Republican and Democratic—against the plans. Regardless of merits, politicos like to back winners. Though specific leaders might take strong public positions in favor, they could not even carry their clubs with them. This was apparent in St. Louis County, where the protagonists of change had a good early opportunity of carrying both the League of Municipalities and the political clubs. As the campaign progressed, however, they had to fight desperately to prevent strong votes in opposition from their own organizations. (And the League of Municipalities did go on record against the plan—though many abstained). Late in the campaign a stalwart protagonist described the situation in his area.

The Creve Cour Township Democratic Club won't go for it at all, though I'm Vice-President and Carol is Treasurer. Our Committeeman was for it too, but the most he could do was stave off a vote. At a big meeting recently with about 150 present they were very hostile—the patronage boys, the County employees, were most hostile toward it. I hope we can forestall a marked ballot against it. (Why do the patronage boys oppose it?) Well, Jim McNary's dead set against it. (Author's note: McNary is County Supervisor.) Funny thing about Jim—I've heard no one speak respectfully of him, but he won—and that's what counts. (How about other elected officials in the county?) They generally oppose it,—and each office has its own patronage.

In short, the opposition, in central city and suburb, was simply the *status quo* mobilized. The extensive network of voluntary organizations and professional communities, the "parapolitical system" of the suburbs, was a readymade communications channel. The municipalities, with specialized personnel committed to their maintenance, dominated the public discourse in the localities. This discourse was further edited by the community newspapers, which had the effect of (1) reflecting messages back to the population and (2) magnifying the aesthetic impact in the process. This easily created an atmosphere, in the suburbs, where it appeared that *nobody* supported the plan except the big city dailies. Thus the distinction between "we" and "they" probably carried along many persons who had little notion of the plan's merits.

The dailies, however, were not powerful protagonists of the plan. Though the editorial officers, as executives of an areawide business situated in the central city, were strong supporters of the plan, the working press was another matter. The journalists who covered local news were part of the free-floating intelligentsia of local government. They were also committed to their working relationships with various *incumbent* political actors. They tended to side against the plans for the latter reason and to justify this partisan position to other intel-lectuals by detailed arguments about the drafting of the plan, the philosophy of municipal government, the ideology of the National Municipal League, and so forth. The practical consequences were rather comical. The editorial pages, read by a minority of the citizens, were overwhelmingly in favor of the plans. The news columns, most widely read, carried stories by writers committed to "tell both sides." In the process, the proponents of the Plan actually created the format, the dramatics, and the space, for their opposition.

Nor should this really surprise us. Resistance to change, on the part of a system, is one indication that it *is* a system.

In summary, then, those persons most committed to the metropolitan revolution were independent of the existing party machine. They were loners if they ranked high in local politics (Porter in Cleveland or Cervantes in St. Louis), but they were preponderantly on the margins of the regular business of politics. They included a disproportionate number of the amateurs for good government, and less than their share of the politically knowledgeable. They had, in their camp, however, the major symbols of civic virtue and the major newspapers.

Their opponents were drawn from the bureaucracy of the central city and from the elected officials of suburbia. Their symbols were the repre-sentatives of "friends and neighbors," and their media were the sub-urban community press and the news columns of the dailies. Their tacit allies were the existing political party officials, whose general suspicion of structural change was never overcome by the protagonists of metro-politan government. Most committed among the regular leaders were those who stood to lose administrative (and patronage) empires and those who stood to lose representation—as was true of the Negro coun-cilmen in Cleveland and in St. Louis.

Thus the personnel drawn into the battle insured a particular kind of a campaign. It was to be largely nonpartisan, with little precinct work and with a great emphasis on the mass media and face-to-face debates before uncommitted audiences. It was a talking campaign, not a pressure campaign.

3

The Train of Events, or

One Thing Leads to Another

We have said that the common political culture sets limits on what may be communicated among political leaders, and between them and the voters. In attempting to understand political change in America, however, it is not enough just to spell out this vocabulary. There is, for example, evidence that public health service for the aged is widely supported by the citizens, yet the program is difficult to put into effect; there is evidence that a large proportion of the citizens oppose aspects of the Bill of Rights, yet the courts continue to honor it. In short, between the flux of opinion based on the political culture and the authoritative statements of law lies a hiatus.

The constitutional-legal armature is relatively static, and yet it is controlling. Political action depends on the constitutional frame and is supported by it. Law is, in effect, a "freezer" of norms from the political culture. Once a given norm has been selected from all logical possibilities and given constitutional status, it becomes difficult to change. This is particularly true of changes aimed at creating metropolitan government, for the "rules of the game" are in the state constitution—in whose definition the municipality is a creature of the state government. To change that constitution requires influence far outside the arena of the metropolitan complex: one must move through the state legislature, then win a statewide referendum. In each of our three cities, the "rural-urban" schism, however real in fact, was considered a near-fatal handicap in winning statewide referenda. As one official in Miami remarked:

(The Dade County delegation) is the "bastard at the family reunion" up at Tallahassee. There's been no special legislation for Dade since the home rule charter . . . People in the State are mostly interested in how much money they can get from Dade. Fourteen counties in Florida pay no taxes and have a majority of their labor force on the public payroll. These are called the "Po'k Chop Counties!"

In the same way, fear of the "Hillbillies up at Jeff City" in St. Louis, and of "downstate Ohio" in Cleveland (which once tried to secede and form the State of Cleveland), continue to exert a limiting effect upon action at the state level.

Then, too, the legal-constitutional system becomes an armature around which grows up the local game of politics. The law and its interpretations set the ground rules for that game, and the interacting players assume those rules. Their own objective security, their hopes of career, and their scoring system all depend upon the given system. Since the interests of incumbents are dependent upon the *status quo*, they are almost uniformly and automatically apt to use their own political weight in preventing change. The existing structure is the condition for their public life: though that life can, in principle, be adapted to a change in constitution, such adaptation may be difficult and costly.

Existing ground rules allow very few strategies for those who wish to change the structure. Assuming four significant levels of action (innovation, persuasion of the voters, change of local law, and change of state constitutional law), the usual strategy is the following: (1) knowledge of the constitutional limits dictates the innovation, which (2) is translated into the political culture of the voters (to the extent it is not controlled by that culture in the first place) and (3) is submitted to their preferences in an election. The constitutional provisions are the "given" within which you work: the problematic is defined within those limits.

In each area the state constitution required appointment or election of a constitutional assembly (called a Charter Commission in Florida and Ohio, a Board of Freeholders in Missouri) for the metropolis. In each area it required a referendum on the issue, and in each area the time intervals were written into the Constitution. Thus once the chain of events was triggered, it had to grind inexorably through the recommendation of the Commission and the referendum election.

In St. Louis the constitutional assembly (or Board of Freeholders) was appointed. Nine members were chosen by judges in the city with the assistance of the mayor, and another nine by judges in the (separate) suburban county with the assistance of the county supervisor; one was chosen by the governor. In Cuyahoga County the slates of nominees for the charter-commission were voted on in a regular election. In Dade County they were chosen by the governor and legislature —but apparently the Dade County delegation was extended legislative courtesy and did the choosing. Each assembly worked for a rigidly limited time period; at the end of that period it *had* to propose a new charter. In St. Louis and in Cuyahoga County the charter had to win majorities of the votes in each area—central city and suburban ring (this meant suburban St. Louis County and Cuyahoga County outside the Cleveland city limits). In Dade County, however, a simple majority of the county voters who participated was adequate.

As we shall see, each set of limits, as well as their variation from metropolis to metropolis in specific requirements, was very important in the ensuing campaign. But first it is necessary to consider the first stage. The innovation process ends with the charter to be submitted; it begins with agitation and a study group.

Metropolitan Agitprop

Each of the metropolitan movements began with a study commission —the Metropolitan St. Louis Survey, the Cleveland METRO Study Commission, the "3-M" study commission of Miami. And each of these study groups, in turn, was created (at least in some peoples' designs) to serve political tactics in the local power play. We shall consider them, briefly, in turn.

In St. Louis a rising young politician, Al Cervantes, had found traffic congestion to be a "live issue." The St. Louis area, with more than 1,500,000 people and 3½ miles of express highway in 1957, was one of the more underdeveloped metropolitan areas in this respect. Consideration of the traffic problem led to the "metropolitan idea," and this in turn led to a more general notion of change. In Cervantes' words:

When I was campaigning for President of the Board of Aldermen back in 1955, I knew the minute my opponent filed that I'd lost. Because he was a damned good man. Now I was in it and I figured I might as well do some good anyway.

It had all started when I tried to get three councilmen each from the city and county together to do something about traffic problems. A reporter told me about this constitutional possibility and I started the move for a new city-county charter. I called a meeting at Medart's Restaurant, in April of 1955. I got the labor guys, the politicians, the Teamsters and others out, and we formed the Citizens Committee for City-County Coordination. The Teamsters helped out and we got out and got our petitions.

Then Tucker—probably because he didn't like me—said the movement was "premature." At that point the Universities under Tucker's influence (or Tucker under their influence, I don't know which) got busy and got the Ford money. They got the survey going. I was against it at first, but then I supported it—and it's been a good thing all along.

Such a chronicle agrees basically with others that have come to our attention.[1]

In one cynical interpretation, "Tucker used the Survey to throw a block into the Citizens Committee." A less cynical and less *ad hominem* interpretation would admit that the survey was a holding action and raise the question: why? One answer is the simple fact of ignorance—little was known of the governmental performances in the area, little of the citizens' response. Further, it was believed by some influential people that a "scientific survey" would increase the odds for achieving

[1] Cf, in particular, *Reform in St. Louis*, Henry J. Schmandt et al, New York: Holt, Rinehart and Winston, 1961.

change through referendum. For both reasons the committee was premature.

In Cuyahoga County, a long history of efforts to consolidate government in the county had taken a new turn as a result of the county officials' growing willingness to accept such a change. It had become apparent that consolidation would not shake Democratic control. An effort was made in 1955 to change the charter in such a way as to allow radical reorganization of county offices by administrative decision. This effort was related to rivalry between the Democratic "regulars," who controlled the county government and the "independent" Democratic mayor. Opposition to this by the county commissioners was combined with a statement of willingness to support a full study of local governmental needs. The study commission aimed at creation of consensus within the framework of "objective analysis" and was supported by all interested parties, including the political regulars.[2] Eventually, with Ford Foundation help, a budget of around $500,000 was attained for the study. Seventy per cent of the budget was from local sources, however—an indication of indigenous support.

In Miami, dissatisfaction with local government had reached an extreme point. In 1953, the voters came within 800 votes of abolishing the City of Miami and consolidating it with the County of Dade. City of Miami officials were, naturally, made anxious by this event. They put up $50,000 for a general study of the governmental needs of the greater Miami area. In the words of one local official:

Well, it was a dirty trick on the pols—they didn't understand what they created when they built the Charter Board. In 1953 . . . the city officials had had the hell scared out of them. They put up the $50,000 for the 3-M Board and the Public Administration Service study—then the study said some kind of Metro government was necessary. You see, the city boys were looking for a way out.

[2] For a detailed discussion of its origins, aims, and the consequences of those aims, see Matthew Holden, Jr., "Decision-Making on a Metropolitan Government Proposition: The Case of Cuyahoga County, Ohio, 1958-59," unpublished Ph.D. Dissertation, Northwestern University Department of Political Science, June, 1961, Chapter III.

The 3-M board didn't represent the politicians though. It represented good government people, the civic leaders, and so on. The politicians were just interested in getting a good press—not realizing the Board would go so far with it. But one thing they didn't want was *consolidation.*

The near miss in abolishment of the city, as Edward Sofen puts it, "convinced many of the adherents of autonomous city government that the only way they could resist complete consolidation and preserve the identity of the municipalities was to work out some compromise formula." [3] The result was the 3-M study board, which hired the Public Administration Service to do the study just noted.

Thus in each case a politically complex and ambiguous situation, in which a move for metropolitan government threatened at least some interests in the local power situation, led to the creation of a study commission delegated to study, objectively, the entire problem of area-wide government.

In St. Louis the metropolitan survey group, formally under a board of directors representing St. Louis and Washington Universities, was in fact autonomous. There was little social interaction with those representing political interests of the area, beyond speeches to the League of Women Voters and a few conferences with civic leaders of various grades. The study group was precisely what it claimed to be, an objective, fact-finding organization. It produced two public reports in 1957 and went out of business.[4] Its reports were given wide publicity by the daily newspapers.

In Cleveland, the "Metro" project produced a long series of study papers, under the aegis of a number of separate citizen's study groups. Metro kept a continual barrage of publicity aimed at the citizens through its coverage by the daily papers; it also acted to coopt some important local political actors into the movement; in the process, it probably educated some localites. It continually emphasized the *local* nature of its problem finding and its putative problem solving.[5]

[3] Edward Sofen, "Problems of Metropolitan Leadership: The Miami Experience," *Midwest Journal of Political Science,* Vol. V, No. 1, February, 1961, page 24.
[4] *Background for Action* and *Path of Progress for Metropolitan St. Louis* (both). St. Louis: Metropolitan St. Louis Survey, 1957.
[5] Holden, *op. cit.,* Chapter II.

The 3-M board in Dade County included a wide array of civic notables—bankers, labor leaders, League of Women Voters' members, mayors of suburban municipalities, executives in the mass media industries. As one ex-member remarked, "We spent a good deal of time going over it with professionals, the PAS from Chicago and the local professionals and lawyers." In the process, some of the fangs of potential opposition were pulled.

Some of the critics fought it and they were right (if I hadn't been on the Charter Board I'd have fought it myself.) If I hadn't been on the Charter Board I'd have killed it. So would Philips, the Mayor of Coral Gables. (*Protocol* of interview with a major mass media executive.)

Thus the Charter Board in Miami, rather than acting as an objective research project, was basically a structure for political indoctrination and organization.

Each study group had produced a set of recommendations for the governmental future of the metropolitan area. Each had recommended a metropolitan government—a new metropolitan district government in St. Louis, and a modified urban county government in the other two areas. Each claimed some measure of objective, scientific status for its report, just as each gained through the halo of "outside experts" on the study group. Let us examine the exact status of these documents.

Political Culture and Political Science

The reports of the three study groups bear a family likeness. Each begins with a rather careful description of the existing governmental structure of the metropolis, with an emphasis upon its service-providing agencies. These are subjected to a critical analysis, and action is recommended.

Indeed, the rationale for the studies rested upon belief that the existing governmental system was inadequate to provide services. Thus the government is first dismembered into its various markets: sewerage, water supply, police protection, and so forth. Each is then subjected to a cost benefit analysis, and each is then surveyed as it varies among the governmental units of the area. In many cases, some supposedly general standard (The National Educational Association's rating of public schools, for example) is used to evaluate local consumer articles. Finally, the investigators ask: what would a given minimal level of services require? Here the answers must be in terms of (*a*) taxing power, (*b*) public borrowing power for capital improvement, and (*c*) extension of legal powers other than fiscal—the police power, the right of public development. In short, the answers include (1) extension of police and fiscal powers to local government *in toto* and (2) transferring some powers to other units (specifically, centralizing them in a new areawide district government).

The second and more dramatic aspect of the reports is their recommendations for action. Each recommends a reordering of the local governmental structure in the light of the requirements deduced in the earlier pages: each, in short, recommends metropolitan government. Because of the anticipated resistance to such drastic change, however, each study group evaluated the "new order" in the light of its probable electability in referendum elections. Thus the recommendations are for "the one best way" to solve the government problems of the metropolis within the given framework of the state constitution and, therefore, in the light of the assumed political tendencies of the electorate.[6] The final recommendations of the study group are a call to *practical political action*. They are given legitimacy and weight by the "expert," "objective," and "scientific" nature of the arguments made for them and the evidence upon which they rest.

In what sense can such recommendations be scientific? Certainly, the descriptive survey of governments satisfies some of the requirements of scientific description. Though thorny problems emerge when one attempts to compare service agencies by the "quality" of their products, such comparison is in principle possible with a high degree of reliability. Certainly it is possible to perform fiscal arithmetic, to estimate costs by projecting from the known to the unknown. And, within the fiscal strait jacket where local governments typically operate (deriving from state constitutional limits), one can calculate the possible sources of revenue,

---

[6] Cf. *Exploring the Metropolitan Community*, Bollens, op. cit., Part 2.

just as one can derive (from the requirements of a service) the new police powers needed to extend and elaborate that service. Such research is simply descriptive, simply logical.

When we seek the "one best way" of attaining governmental change, however, the scientific validity of the venture is in great doubt. First, it is clear that our knowledge of the "electability" of charters in referenda leaves much to be desired. After all, most of the plans turned down recently (including the Cuyahoga County Charter and the St. Louis Metropolitan District Plan) rest upon the judgment of such experts. The crude pragmatic argument should be given weight. The truth is, the political process in a metropolis is hardly understood when it is invoked by such recurrent and massively studied elections as that for President of the United States: it is a dark continent indeed where referenda are concerned. Thus the recommendations of the "experts" on political feasibility are at best informed guesswork, at worst shots in the dark.

Second, the entire question of reordering government in this way for these ends is not amenable to scientific determination. It rests upon implicit assumptions as to what government should do for the population, what distribution of costs and benefits is morally right, what kind of city should be encouraged to develop on this site, what kind of life is proper to urban man. Neither the Purification Rites, the Fertility Rites, nor the drive for efficiency in government, are equally attractive, or pressing to all citizens. This is, in fact, what elections are about. The most that the study group's report can really say is: *If* you agree with the aims assumed in the first part of our report, *and* you accept our judgment about the political process in this area, *then* our recommendations are (we think) the way to achieve those aims.

For some political actors this is perfectly adequate. Many others misunderstand the report and take it as analogous to a physician's diagnosis of a sick patient. Many others see it as near-quackery. And some people think it is "scientific" and hate it for that reason. Though the official response to the report, given by newspapers and civic leaders, tends to be pontifically positive, under the surface many are not certain. And few understand. "This," as one campaigner said, pointing to the St. Louis report, "is the Bible."

Finally, we might ask, did the reports' recommendations have any effect? There is some doubt on this score. The ex-Mayor of Miami, one of the more potent political figures, put it this way:

So the city appropriated $50,000, and formed the 3-M study board, and hired PAS and so forth. I've always felt that was pretty immaterial, but they brought out reports and kinda educated the people.

Again, however, the crude pragmatic test is relevant. Each of the charters submitted in referenda complied essentially with the recommendations of the study groups. But rather than seeing this as a simple cause and effect relationship, it is more accurate to see the study groups as already committed to action within the constitutional framework. In Cleveland the urban county was agreed upon in principle by all interested parties favoring Metro government *before* the charter commission was elected. In Miami the study board was, precisely, a compromise between consolidation and the *status quo*. Only in St. Louis was there doubt as to the course the board of freeholders should take. In that case, it is likely the report was of some importance, reflecting, however, the political anarchy of that board. In the other cities the aims of the study groups were so similar to those of the charter commission that the similarity in their findings is no surprise. We shall consider the matter further; first, it is necessary to discuss the three constitutional assemblies.

The Constitutional Assemblies

The report of the St. Louis survey was released in August, 1957. Two years and two months later a referendum was finally held on the Metropolitan District Plan Charter. First the petitions gathered by the Citizens Committee for City-County Partnership were partially invalidated. Then, in May, the Board of Freeholders was appointed. It sat for a year, and the election took place six months later.

The Board of Freeholders was generally nonpartisan, though it ended up with nine Democrats, eight Republicans, and two independents.

More important, however, it did not represent leadership in the area. As Schmandt describes it:

> Most of the members were unknown to a wide public audience and few of them were recognized as community leaders. No one of major stature in local government and politics was included among the appointees; neither was the elite of the local business structure. The influential Civic Progress, Incorporated, and the top leadership of the Chamber of Commerce were not included. Key officials of civic organizations were also missing. Only the officialdom of the unions was well represented.[7]

This is, indeed, a curious body to represent a metropolitan area as it approaches radical change. Schmandt does not, however, believe this indicates a plan to "sink" the charter. Instead, he speaks of the "haphazard selection process" (judges, Mayor, Supervisor, and Governor), the cost in time to those who accepted the appointment, the prolonged waiting period which "dispelled any sense of urgency on the part of those who might have been concerned about the choice of freeholders."[8] In his words, there was only a "slight degree of concern displayed by major interest groups in the matter of appointments."[9] Lack of interest and ineptitude, within a prescribed system of "politically random" selection, may do as descriptive terms for the process.

In Cleveland a few members of the Metro study group were instrumental in forcing early election of a charter commission. They succeeded in getting an election in November, 1958 (while the Metro group was still at work). In the election the regular Democratic party put up a slate, as did the Republicans, and several minor slates were entered. The commission that emerged was one heavily weighted with powerful "regular" Democratic party "pros"—though without representation from the Lausche-Celebrezze wing of the party. Though all members of the commission were not committed to metropolitan gov-

---

[7] *Reform in St. Louis*, page 13.
[8] *Ibid.*, page 14.
[9] *Ibid.*, page 14. Mayor Tucker told an interviewer afterward that he did not get even *one* representative for his position on the Board of Freeholders.

ernment, most were. Those who were thought of it in terms of a "federal" system, an urban county which would leave the municipalities standing but bring many major powers within the county offices. At least three, and possibly five, members of the commission would have liked the job of county executive had the charter passed.[10]

In Miami, the 3-M study board (Metropolitan Miami Municipal Board) remained in being after the publication of its report in 1954.[11] This report, written by Public Administration Service personnel, formed the basis for the new charter (also written by PAS). As Sofen remarks, the PAS provided "the 'Good Housekeeping Seal of Approval' for Miami's Metropolitan experiment." [12] Thus the interim from study to the submission of the charter was not one of "metro in vacuo"; the group that supported change rallied around the 3-M board and were given continuous publicity by the press.

The Florida Home Rule amendment, allowing a metropolitan charter, was passed in November, 1956. The governor appointed the Charter Commission immediately (with the aid of Senator Gautier and the Dade County delegation) and, with the aid of PAS, a charter was readied in what must be a record time. As for the charter board members, they somewhat resembled those in St. Louis. Most of them were suburban officials, professional persons, and owner-entrepreneurs. The lack of political leaders, however, is simply a result of the political flux in the Dade County area; nothing comparable to the "regular Democratic party" structure in Cuyahoga exists in Dade. Nor, on the other hand, do vast economic empires; in Dade County a company employing 200 persons is a very large enterprise. The Charter Board members represented, fairly well, the reputational hierarchy of the metropolitan area. But it was representation by *sampling*, not by delegated power.[13]

---

[10] Holden, *op. cit.*, Chapter III.
[11] *The Government of Metropolitan Miami*, Chicago: Public Administration Service, 1954.
[12] Sofen, *op. cit.*, page 26.
[13] Sofen, *op. cit.*, page 33.

The Deliberations of the Assembly

The Constitutional Assembly is charged with a task somewhat like that of a jury. It finds fact and urges decision. But its job is even more difficult, for it must work in an area where complex causal structures are assumed, where complex (and often contradictory) goals are defined, and where the relationship between cause and effect, structure and goal, must be determined. From the effects of different representational schemes to the consequences of given tax policies, it faces some of the most vexing questions of political science. From the decision as to the proper aims of government to the protection of individual freedom of choice, it confronts some of the most complex value questions in the realm of public discourse.

Nor does it have the advantages of the jury where organization is concerned. Instead of a rigid assignment of duties, a limited place within a continuing, rationalized, and professionalized system, its role system is completely undefined and its relationships with the outside world problematic. Even such basic matters as choosing its own organizational structure and defining its agenda are unspecified: the political culture requires the constitutional assembly but provides no rules for its operation.

It is implicit, in the great powers designated to such assemblies, that they should in fact produce a finding. (Indeed, the Missouri constitution apparently *requires* agreement on a new charter from the Board of Freeholders). If one could resurrect the political culture of the past now frozen in the legal provisions for such assemblies, assumptions of this nature would seem to emerge: (1) A dozen or so citizens, good men and true, *can* represent the chief interests which should be considered in drafting a constitution; (2) they will indeed *do* so, through the sheer fact of common membership in the assembly and responsibility for its product; (3) in the process, major conflicts will be accommodated; (4) this will be continually related to the opinion of the populace, through the devices of public hearings and other forms of publication; (5) so that the new charter will be a reasonable plan for the government of the locality.

In fact, few of these assumptions held in the St. Louis board's career. The ill-assorted and mutually unacquainted personnel showed little attention to the organizational facts of life. One of the least politically experienced members was made chairman. The operating rules allowed almost complete freedom in proposing, in clique organization, in debate. They also allowed free communication with outsiders. (For a time the Board of Freeholders held its meetings on television). The rules opened meeting after meeting to representatives of various interests who were heard. Such "hearings" in fact interfered with the basic work schedule of the board, cutting down greatly the time needed for the free interchange of ideas and the compromise that is implicit in assembling representatives of widely differing views.

Nor did the St. Louis board call upon the expertise of the local social scientists who had prepared the reports of the survey. Indeed, there was a leaning over backward to avoid the use of these resources. While a few members "accepted most of the research findings of the Survey . . . and . . . seemed to believe that little purpose would be served by reexamining the same problems," the dominant group "insisted that the initial round of hearings should concentrate on ascertaining how citizens and public officials regarded the problems and needs of the metropolitan area." [14] The board repeated, with amateur tactics, work that had been carried out systematically a year and a half earlier. Finally, since the spokesmen for the community yielded nothing but repeating results (and results congruent with survey findings), the board turned to its assignment, the drafting of a charter.

Lacking a given structure, lacking an organization through their previous associations and political commitments, the St. Louis board was an extreme example of what Holden calls "primitive uncertainty." [15] The process by which it chose a chairman was comical; his weakness was a logical result. In this power vacuum, what little alignment was possible on broader and more permanent bases intruded into the board's organization, structuring the interchange of notions and resulting in a dramatic split. Briefly, the city representatives and the

[14] Schmandt, *op. cit.*, page 17.
[15] Holden, *op. cit.*

union leaders organized early in favor of all-out merger of city and suburbs. One may speculate about the reasons; certainly the original movement had been slanted towards merger, and certainly city politicians preferred merger to other possible plans. The labor leaders, in turn, were closely tied in with the city politicos through their ongoing, day-to-day business. (The chief labor leader, Farris, was important because of his association with the head of labor's Committee on Political Education.) And, within the unstructured discourse of the board, these alignments led early to a self-reinforcing system. Mutual aid, differential association among the cliques, and conflict with the opposition resulted in a rigidly "pro-merger" position.

The suburban representatives, willing at first to consider compromise, drifted slowly towards a position in favor of "federalism," or a metropolitan district. They believed "merger" to be out of the question politically; it was unelectable. (Nor did they ever manifest much taste for it). However, the nearly even split on the board did not lead either faction to attempt compromise. So certain were the "mergerites" of victory that they could not be bothered; their rigidity, in turn, produced withdrawal among the "federationists." Polarization resulted between the two cliques.

One of the board members, a suburban lawyer who later campaigned for the district plan, described it this way.

The five man drafting committee that wrote the District Plan had little help from the other fourteen members. Both plans—this and merger—were completely written up before the board voted. Theirs was all printed up—they were terribly proud of it and sure it would pass, and I guess they got a little overconfident.

Question: Did they really think merger would pass in the county?

They just knew they'd get it through the Board. They got real cocky and lost some support that way. As to what would happen at the polls in the county—they just stuck their heads in the sand on that one. McRoberts (consulting attorney) said, by the way, that *their* plan is much shakier than ours from a legal point of view. He drafted a version for them, but they rewrote it because his was dull.

The board first met on May 19, 1956; on April 15, 1957, the board voted for the District Plan by a 10 to 9 vote. The hard core of the "mergerites" refused to sign the final plan. The same board member commented on the results of the board's decision.

When we took the decisive vote we had fifteen days before signing it for revision. We had been revising right along before the vote. I anticipated a fight after the vote, that they would have a real voice in changing our plan. But by and large they didn't care at all. I tried to get them interested— though my associates thought I was foolish to ask for sabotage—but they didn't care. (Why not?) I don't know—I guess they figured they'd go out and fight it—and a lot of them sure did.

The St. Louis Board of Freeholders is a good example of the way complex deliberative assemblies can operate when manned by "average, intelligent people" who have neither political experience nor party responsibilities. There is no evidence that the board was swung at the mercy of outside currents; indeed, as Schmandt puts it,

Even the labor representatives, while reflecting the biases of their organizational affiliations, were left free to formulate their own policy. Careful probing and interviewing failed to reveal any evidence of covert attempts to influence the board. The major interest groups followed a "hands off" policy, showing little concern over the board's activities.[16]

Instead, the board was swung by the vagaries of personal competence (and incompetence), prejudice, clique formation, and folk political science.

The Cuyahoga Board was in some respects the diametrical opposite. Though it, too, was the victim of "primitive uncertainty," this chaos was resolved through everyday channels—appeal to the boss of the regular Democratic party, Ray Miller. Its organizational structure was then patterned on regular legislative strategies; the preponderance of Democratic political actors guaranteed the success of the move. Well-known and accepted norms allowed a central structure of control and

---

[16] *Reform in St. Louis, op. cit.*, page 33. Schmandt and his associates perform a useful "cluster analysis of paired voting" to test further the nature of position formation and change (Chapter III, *Ibid.*) It supports the above statements.

a *modus vivendi.* This took the form of a "drafting committee," which included the politically ambitious; a Republican, a liberal Democrat, one representative of the Cleveland City Council, and a major figure from the regular Democrats who was also chairman of the commission. Notably missing from this committee was the one representative of Mayor Celebrezze—Rogers, the port commissioner. Many major decisions were made by an informal "executive committee." The remaining members of the Charter Commission had relatively little effect on key issues; most of them went along with the executive committee decisions, for they were, after all, actors in the Democratic party organization of the area that had elected them to the commission.[17]

The Cuyahoga commission's working rules placed a heavy emphasis on the secret caucus. This operated, first, to keep the work of the drafting committee secret from the remainder of the commission, and second, to insulate the commission from public response. The first trial draft was presented as a "talking paper" to the public. For this reason, few took it seriously, and the early public hearings were sparse and poorly attended. *Within* the commission, however, it became the basis for political negotiation and compromise. Thus by the time the final draft was ready for public hearings, key members of the commission were no longer willing to revise it: internal consensus would have been placed in hazard.

The Cuyahoga commission also worked in a vacuum—not a power vacuum, but an information vacuum. The politicians, suspicious of civic entrepreneurs and men of good will, had kept control firmly in the hands of the regular Democratic party. They had cemented that control by a secrecy rule. Certain disasters, however, stemmed directly from this organization of work. Within the commission's key committee, the chief argument was one between a "hard charter" which would take great power from other bodies and give it to the new county and a "soft charter" which would conciliate existing power blocs through making minimal changes. The regular politicians tended to support the former, the civic entrepreneurs the latter. Conflict on

---

[17] These and following observations are largely based upon Holden, *op. cit.*, supplemented by intensive interviews in Cuyahoga County in Winter, 1959–1960.

the issue, however, tended to define it as all or nothing. Little attention was paid to the rank order of the power blocs to be accommodated and the relative cost of accommodation. In fact, Negro citizens were to be relieved of their relative representational weight—and Negro votes "sank the charter" in Cleveland. Airports and harbors were to become county property without a referendum—and the director of this agency, though a member of the commission, did not sign the product and fought vigorously against the charter in the campaign. Civic assets in the suburbs would be transferred without compensation, although the Metro study had recommended they remain separate.

Such decisions can be seen as predictable from the dominance of Democratic regulars in the commission. However, the general isolation of the commission from the metropolitan population and its reliance upon "folk political science" in estimating its electoral chances led to further tactical errors. One major provision of the charter effectively destroyed Civil Service protection for public employees. This provision antagonized the Civil Service League, and word was circulated to the entire 20,000 public employees in the area. It was a strong argument for the Negro opponents of the charter ("our people rely pretty heavily on those Civil Service rules in getting and keeping jobs and getting promoted"), and it raised eyebrows among the partisans of improved mechanical efficiency in government. Yet it was not seriously debated in the commission. The drafters seemed to assume it was non-controversial—or worth doing no matter what the cost. When a staff member asked, "But won't that leave employees no protection from their boss?" the answer was, "That's right! No protection! We don't want them to have any." (A general hubbub of agreement from the gentlemen assembled.) Such a scene indicates the kind of folly possible when a few men, isolated, interact intensely with respect to issues which are never checked against any particular social reality. (It also reminds one of the Mad Hatter's tea party—"No room! No room!") As Holden puts it, little effort was made to differentiate between political and technical problems, and there was a "marked disposition to rely on the decision-maker's personal knowledge and sources." [18] As

[18] Holden, *op. cit.*, pp. 323-324.

consensus was developed during the course of the commission's meetings, better information was, in fact, a potential danger. Thus, "As decision time came closer to expiration, decision-makers were less and less willing to consider the objective consequences of their actions." [19]

In Dade County the Charter Board was appointed in November, 1956. It produced its document in rapid order, and the charter was submitted in a referendum in May, 1957. The board could move quickly because it could assume consensus, emerging from the long-term discussion of the issue in the 3-M study group, from the terms of the Home Rule amendment which indicated some form of urban county government, and from the use of PAS as a professional drafting body. Though the board had important advantages, it did not have much leeway for public hearings. They were described by one political notable as follows:

There was enough politicking to introduce a lot of language which kept the document from being as near perfect as I felt it should be. Because of time—they finished four days before their legal deadline—they only held five public meetings in different parts of town. Finally then, at the end of each speech, the citizens would have three minutes to discuss the Charter. It was more of a compliance with forms of democratic process than a real one.

More important to the Miami Charter Board was the long series of discussions and negotiations that had taken place on the 3-M Board. The same informant continues:

We had representatives from the different cities on the 3-M Board and we tried to get everybody to agree—used decorative language which lulled them into a belief (I think because they weren't educated) that things would remain as they were.

In general, the Dade County Board was relatively pacific. Its operations seem to reflect a consensus on metropolitan government, arrived at as a halfway house between the consolidation feared by City Halls and the existing discontent with government among the civic entre-

---

[19] *Loc. cit.*

preneurs. The mass media, most of the city fathers and the "experts" of local government were all on one side. The few who were opposed— the Dade County League of Municipalities, for example—kept quiet. The enemies were not represented in the charter commission phase.

The Products

A new constitution is both a bargaining instrument and an effort to reshape the existing bargaining advantages of a governmental area. In the same way, a charter commission is both a body of citizens finding new ways to achieve old goals (or new goals) and a set of plenipotentiaries for the various political interests of the area. Both the artifact and the actors who produced it are important in the ensuing political career of the charter.

The St. Louis charter specified a metropolitan district, with overriding governmental powers in seven areas. These included transportation, traffic, planning, industrial development, sewerage, civil defense, and property assessment. All other powers were to be retained by the local municipalities and special district governments. The new district would thus provide a new level of government for the area, creating a rival head (in the district president, elected at large) to the existing political panjandrums, and a rival legislature (in the district council, elected partly by districts, partly at large) to those of the City of St. Louis, St. Louis County, and the various municipalities. It would have duplicated some agencies that already existed, by separating "local" and "metropolitan" functions—traffic arteries and zoning were two such tasks. Though its original budget would have been small (nobody estimated the millage would yield over $20,000,000 per year), it could expand its budget through service charges, revenue bond issues, and tax increases by referendum. Being a "partisan" government it would, presumably, reflect the existing balance of power between Democrats and Republicans—a balance increasingly in favor of the Democratic party throughout the metropolitan area.

The Cuyahoga County Charter would have given the urban county overriding powers in fourteen areas.[20] Its greater extension reflected the combination of existing county powers with those of the new government. It also reflected the victory of the "hard charter" party (the regular Democrats) on the commission—and a general belief that the charter would pass. The county could take over municipally owned property lying within its legally defined functions for compensation determined by a process of bargaining capped with provision for arbitration. The county would, as in St. Louis, be presided over by a metropolitan executive (elected at large) and a Metropolitan Assembly of Cuyahoga County (with nine members elected at large and ten elected from five assembly districts). The charter would, finally, abolish most elective offices in the county. This government would also be "partisan" and, again, Cuyahoga County had been heavily Democratic for some time.

The Dade County Charter was even more inclusive than that of Cuyahoga County.[21] In addition to the regular governmental functions it gave the new county control over changes in municipal boundaries. It was to be governed by a Board of County Commissioners, including one from each of five districts elected by the voters of that district, one from each district elected by the voters of Dade County as a whole, and one from each municipality of 60,000 or more population. No municipalities were to be abolished, but their powers were drastically reduced in principle; minimum standards for their services could be

[20] Sanitary sewerage and storm drainage, water supply, roads and highways, public assistance and poor relief, mass transit, airports, ports and harbors, the zoo, civil defense, air and water pollution control, refuse disposal, public health, metropolitan area planning and metropolitan parks. The new county would also have concurrent powers over police records and building codes. (Proposed Home Rule Charter for Cuyahoga County, Ohio, submitted the 30th of August, 1959.)

[21] Transportation, traffic, transit, terminals and ports, police and fire training, communication, and records, planning, health and hospitals, parks, playgrounds and the like, housing, urban renewal, and the like, sewerage and waste collections, zoning and business regulation, as well as more general fiscal powers. (*The Charter of Metropolitan Dade County, Florida*, adopted May 21, 1957.)

set by the county, and their officials would obviously suffer in power and prestige. The Dade County Charter, however, did not provide for an elected political head; instead, an appointed county manager was provided. The elections in the county were to be nonpartisan. Thus the existing nonpartisan fluidity was to be retained in the new metropolitan government. Other elective offices of the old county government were abolished, leaving only the Metropolitan government and the municipal offices for aspiring local politicians.

Each of these proposed charters would have effected a radical change in the distribution of power in a metropolis. They would have injured certain corporate interests, by transfers of taxing and police power (the central city, the suburbs, the special districts); they would have injured the careers of specific office holders, by transferring assets, administrative empires, prestige, to others; they would have strengthened political rivals by improving the prestige and visibility of their jobs. What did they offer in return?

In St. Louis, there was a sustained effort to minimize the losses to the corporate entities, central city and suburbs. The district plan was, in fact, to leave the sleeping dogs alone. As Eliot has said, of the recommendation made by the Metropolitan St. Louis Survey:

> The Survey's members weighed the urgency of change against the difficulties of achieving it, and agreed on that course which seemed to them necessary and reasonably possible of acceptance.[22]

Such was the thinking of the "federationists" on the Board of Freeholders. They felt that many influential persons opposed merger, and constantly sought "to legitimize or support their position by referring to the survey's conclusions and the 'experts' who conducted the study."[23] Their belief was, in fact, shared by Cervantes, with special reference to the City of St. Louis. Originally sponsoring the movement for merger, Cervantes became the leader of the campaign for the District Plan. Towards the end of that campaign he said:

[22] Thomas H. Eliot, "Dilemmas in Metropolitan Research," *Midwest Journal of Political Science*, February, 1958, p. 37.
[23] Schmandt, *op. cit.*, page 18.

Merger wouldn't go. You'd have nothing but rabid opposition everywhere. In the City your pols would know it'd shake their jobs. That's how we beat the Charter you know—those guys got out and sweated for that one.

Thus the St. Louis plan did not remove anyone from office. It took powers (though many were unused) from municipalities, it preempted some of the "scarce tax dollar"—but it changed no governmental boundary or political office. It did impose *areawide obligations* for services upon municipalities that already provided those services for their citizens. As we shall see, this became an important issue. And it did create a major metropolitan elected office, one which might well tower above that of Mayor of St. Louis in the eyes of the interested; this may also have been important.

The Cuyahoga charter, much stronger in its effects, also sidestepped existing governments. It did abolish important elective offices at the county level; more important, it transferred enormous capital assets from municipalities to the county (including the lucrative Cleveland water supply system and the Shaker Heights Rapid Transit system) and in the process handed over "empires" to the metropolitan executive. In exchange for these, other swaps were made: the county would, for example, accept the expensive responsibility for poor relief. Though no existing offices were to be abolished, the *meaning* would be changed with the transfer of powers to the new county. Thus representation in that county was important, and certain groups (Republicans, Negroes, suburbanites—"the three minorities" as one commission member put it) were likely to be under-represented in the new government. The commission assumed, perhaps, that the interest in "good government" might placate many, and Negroes and Republicans had usually supported metropolitan movements in the past.

In Dade County there was least regard for bargaining. The county charter, in principal, greatly weakened other existing governments and turned the county into a metropolitan municipality. There were, furthermore, many provisions for extending its power further in the future. In the loose, unstructured, "nonpartisan" politics of Dade County, there simply were no party interests to be placated. As Sofen puts it, "Miami with its 'every man for himself' type of politics in effect has a no-party system and, consequently, was spared the kind of struggle that might have occurred if the fate of political parties had turned on the outcome." [24]

Although the charter commissions were oriented to bargaining, in St. Louis and Cuyahoga County particularly, there is little evidence of real "chips down" negotiation. In St. Louis the mayor, along with many, many other people, gave evidence of his opinion at the open hearings conducted by the board. But the vote of the Freeholders was in no sense contingent upon his response. Mayor Celebrezze spoke once in the Cuyahoga commission's hearings—but again, though tentative efforts were made, no genuine agreement was made and perhaps none was sought.[25] Thus the political head of the major governmental unit affected, the major dignitary of the metropolis, was allowed to remain in a very ambiguous position *vis a vis* the new charter. But this, after all, differed only in degree from the commissions' responses to suburban politicians, Negroes, civil service employees, and others. The bargaining of the commissions has been felicitously dubbed "implicit bargaining" by Holden—and such bargaining suffers from its one-way direction, its lack of commitment by the party being wooed. It amounts simply to an effort "to call the shots," to guess which way the political cats will jump. Charter commission members have at their disposal, intellectually, only the tools used in the research reports; they did not use these with much effect, nor did they use their social and political levers to guarantee predictable outcomes.

The badly split Board of Freeholders in St. Louis filed a charter in May, 1959, but it went unsigned by the hard-core mergerites. These men, including the chairman and the labor representatives, had no intention of supporting the District Plan; they became, in fact, a nucleus of opposition to it. As one major leader of the District Plan campaign put it:

[24] Sofen, *op. cit.*, page 20.
[25] In Miami, General Evans, then City Manager of Miami and dubbed by many "the most powerful political figure in town," did not oppose the new metropolitan government. Bargaining was not needed.

The real trouble goes way back to the split on the Board of Freeholders. The labor guys took their position there so hard—and they took it over into the campaign. Then they neutralized the politicians—and we got no support.

The Board of Freeholders in St. Louis did produce several of the leaders in the District Plan campaign, as well as several leaders of its opposition. The fatal split between suburbs and city, reflected in the split between District Plan and merger, resulted in some of the differences aired in the ensuing campaign.

In Cuyahoga County the Charter Commission, chiefly pledged to the Democratic party—and otherwise pledged to metropolitan reform—stayed almost solidly lined up behind their artifact. One major exception, however, was the Director of Ports and Harbors, William J. Rogers, the one commission member who did not sign the charter. A member who had objected to the transfer of his facilities to county government (fruitlessly, as it turned out), a member of the Mayor of Cleveland's administrative team (and considered his representative on the commission), Rogers fought vigorously against the new charter. In Dade County, likewise, the only member of the board who fought the charter was a member of the establishment, George O'Kell, City Attorney for Miami. Otherwise the Charter Board remained staunch in support of the metropolitan government.

Thus the preexisting consensus, in Cleveland and Miami, narrowed greatly the area of possible conflict on their boards. Committed to some form of "halfway house," their problem was one of degree, of specifics. In St. Louis, a Board of Freeholders representing nobody but themselves, with no outside support or constraints, was free to split down the middle. This raised serious doubts, in some people's minds, as to the legitimacy of its product. Yet the split may have been an accurate reflection of opinion in the metropolis.

4

How They Brought
the Good News

It is a long way between proposing and disposing, where the metropolitan revolution is concerned. The proposers, a small sample of the urban complex, interact with each other in relative isolation from the vast majority and the *vox populi*. As we have noted in detail, the charter drafting operations were conducted in near-vacuums; the leaders of the movement for metropolitan government and those who created the instrument of its achievement had little "feedback" from the population for whom it was intended.

In bridging this distance, they assume certain characteristics. They assume, first, the uniformity of the political culture—the equivalence between arguments made in their deliberations (and heard in public hearings) and those considered relevant by the voters. The fertility ritual and the drama of the fight for progress are culture complexes supporting such arguments. In the same way, they assume a political technology—a way of doing things politically—which has a uniform validity as well as communicability.

The political technology assumes a preexisting role system in the political community which can be activated in the given instant. Such a role system must provide an organized body of men, who can stand for (a) one civic agenda, (b) one position on a given issue, and (c) clear and widely shared interests in the political community. These actors must, in turn, order themselves to pose a limited number of alternatives to the voters (*two*, in the American case), interpret these alternatives with respect to the general norms shared by significant parts of the populace, and finally communicate with a significant body of the voters. This they assume will influence them to dispose of the proposition in a meaningful way.

The Campaign for the St. Louis District Plan

In the remainder of this and in the following chapters, we shall be forced to rely most heavily on our St. Louis investigations. We have the advantage of an intensive study of the St. Louis area, and comparable data are not available across the board for the other metropolitan areas. However, we will note congruences and differences wherever possible.

There were many snags in the way of translating the District Plan Charter into a political movement. The move for a new metropolitan government grew out of the ordinary political process in the City of St. Louis. It was thrown first to the scholars of the survey, then to the rank amateurs of the Board of Freeholders. It then had to find its way back to the political professionals—or some alternative set of role-players capable of organizing a campaign on a complex issue for the metropolitan area as a whole.

If one makes a common assumption about the St. Louis metropolis, that it is "controlled by a power structure," the result should be predictable. The notion that great American cities are (1) dominated by a small number of powerful people, who (2) owe their power to economic position and (3) therefore control the political process and call the shots on key issues has been an archetype of American thought. It has lately been given renewed currency in social science by the work of Floyd Hunter.[1] The St. Louis District Plan campaign offers an opportunity to test it.

[1] Floyd Hunter, *Community Power Structure*, University of North Carolina Press, 1953.

If there were a community power structure in the St. Louis area, it could be expected to either (a) favor the plan and see that it carried, (b) oppose the plan and see that it was defeated, (c) take a "hands-off" position and fail to appear in a chronicle of major events. In this case, it was clear that the dominant economic interests, organized in Civic Progress Incorporated, *did* approve the District Plan. They endorsed it shortly after the Board of Freeholders had released it. They also formed a Committee for City-County Partnership, including many civic notables and such major organizations as the Chamber of Commerce. They provided the original and substantial funds. This was to be expected: the District Plan, a relatively mild and very reasonable instrument of change, was legitimized through the morality plays of fertility and increased governmental efficiency—old songs to the economic dominants.

From there on the play did not go according to script. The next steps should have been the translation of "community power" into political power to ensure a favorable result at the polls. This would be expected to take place through (a) pressure on the professional political leaders, who would (b) turn the wheel of the ward machines so that the political structure would move in the same direction as opinion among the civic elite, (c) resulting in a solid front and the conversion of the voters. However, none of the political leaders belonged to the committee, with the single exception of Al Cervantes, who became the campaign chairman for the City of St. Louis. A relatively minor figure took the same post for the county. And, surprising to everyone, no "Big Mule" took the overall chairmanship of the committee. While a chairman was sought among the eligibles, the campaign stalled, *from May until the end of August*. Three months were lost—only two were left. Finally, an automobile dealer, unknown to local politics and of secondary status as civic leader, became general chairman of this arduous campaign.

Nor is there any evidence that the Civic Progress group ever put pressure on the political heads. The Mayor of St. Louis, Raymond Tucker, had been supported for years by this group and had cooperated in building the "St. Louis Renaissance." Yet the mayor's position was not clear at the time Civic Progress endorsed the plan and contributed

$40,000 to the campaign (with the understanding that this was only the beginning). Then later in the campaign, when it could be calculated to do the most damage, the mayor made a forthright and powerful speech opposing the plan and urging the voters to turn it down. Civic Progress, rather than corralling the mayor, seemed instead to be *dependent upon him,* the wind disappeared from its sails at that point, and new money ceased to flow in. (Indeed, some members of Civic Progress indicated that if they had only *known* Tucker was opposed they would never have favored the District Plan in the first place.)

Nor were the political heads who did favor the plan able to use the party machinery of the area. Cervantes was able to line up only three of the 28 wards in the city; Donahue and his associate Daniels had similar success in the county; the mayor of the largest city in the suburban county, and President of the County League of Municipalities, could not carry the League for the plan. (It eventually voted against it.) However, the political leaders opposing the plan did not use the party machinery either: Cervantes is given some credit for neutralizing them, but it is very likely they did not feel it was necessary to fight. Thus the usual machinery for "running a campaign" was stilled: the campaign for the District Plan was carried on over, under, and around the usual party apparatus.

In Cuyahoga County events took, in certain key respects, similar paths. Again, there was a long delay in assembling the leadership of the campaign committee. Again, there was no real effort to coopt the politically popular Mayor of Cleveland, Celebrezze. Again the political machine, even though it was formally committed (through the pressure of the "regular Democrats"), did not fight for the plan. The political boss, given a campaign kitty by the wealthy businessmen favoring the charter, distributed it equally (in $500 shares) to those who supported the charter and those who fought it alike. He then announced that the party did not require a position in favor of the charter: it was up to every man and his conscience.[2] In general, the local councilmen of

[2] This resulted in such absurd contretemps as that forcing the co-chairman for the Charter Campaign (a Republican, Ralph Perk) to fight an opponent financed by the Charter Campaign. The latter campaigned on the slogan "Beat the Charter and Beat Ralph Perk!"

Democratic persuasion simply pocketed the money and took whatever line on the charter seemed to be most popular in their wards. As for the Mayor of Cleveland, like Tucker he eventually took a very strong stand against the new county charter.

In Dade County there were no politicos excepting the "loners" of a nonpartisan electoral game. The mass media and the civic entrepreneurs dominated discourse, and the politicos tended to agree, with the exception of a few civic employees. The campaign was a newspaper and television affair, and the hurdles of St. Louis and Cuyahoga County simply did not exist. Thus the assumptions of a community power structure come closest to fitting in Dade County, the metropolis without a party structure.

The Campaign Strategy

The campaign for the District Plan was conceived and launched by an *ad hoc* committee, a ragged coalition. The choice of top leaders was described by one leader in this fashion:

When I came in, the present campaign leaders were asked to serve by a small group of men who derived their precedent, their jurisdiction, just from their own desires and interest. (Who were they?) Shepley, Chancellor of Washington U., Ed Clark of the telephone company, Kurth of the Chamber of Commerce—And that, by the way, was the last we heard from them except money. We had to put an organization together from scratch. (How much money?) We're not at the end yet, as I understand our situation we have about $60,000 or $70,000 plus pledges and donations. We've had personal help too; the guy who gave us the store for an office didn't care if I wanted to use it for a crap game or what.

James, the chairman, was at least second choice for leadership of the committee. You know, it was a very thin line from that Board of Freeholders to the Citizen's Committee to me. (Why are you doing it?) Well, public interest, I think—at least Jack Daniel and I are. There's nothing in it for a practicing lawyer.

I took on this job because Jack asked me. I don't really know who chose me for the job. I got in and I found we didn't have any organization. We had to start from scratch. We haven't much staff and we are having to work against a real short time period for the campaign.

The group which met as the Citizen's Committee on May 22 immediately after the board released the charter delayed the choice of a Chairman until August 28, then passed the decision to a small nucleus of young politicians and aspirants.

These men represented the "politically savvy" part of the coalition. They were either professionals out to improve their game or young liberals anxious to fight for a good cause (and a career to boot). Other members of the coalition included the "good government gals," the League of Women Voters; Civic Progress Incorporated, representing the large economic interests of the area; the Chambers of Commerce and other businessmen's fraternities; certain professional societies—planners, architects, and the like; and the Building Trades Council of the AFL-CIO, anxious to increase building activity in the area. This was the organizational support of the District Plan.

The campaign was organized according to a fairly clear pattern. First it was divided into two different operations. That in the central city was headed by Al Cervantes, President of the Board of Aldermen and long a leader in the metropolitan movement. In the county, a separate organization was headed by Donahue, a promising young lawyer identified with the Democratic party. The rationale behind this, as interpreted by one leader, was as follows:

Well I don't know, exactly; it was in existence when I came in. You conduct different campaigns in the city and in the county—because there's a certain amount of provincial feeling. If a city man tried to pursuade the county, or *vice versa*, there would be an amount of resistance. There is resistance anyway.

Then in the city you have the ward organizations, while in the county we have a weak township-based machine, but many other organizations. A political approach through the municipalities is stronger than a party approach in the county—so you need knowledge of the different parts of the area.

My experience in county municipality work (as attorney S.G.) is probably one of the things that might qualify me for this particular job. That is, there's something to know about how one would act in Webster Groves, in Brentwood, in Kirkwood. The type of guy to line up and the kinds of things one has to say and do.

Donahue was helped consistently and energetically by Jackson Daniel, the young Democratic lawyer who had been with Cervantes in the Citizen's Committee in 1956.

The Means of Persuasion. The nature of the man and woman power available limited the kind of campaign that could be carried out. The two-month time period (from August 28 to November 3) also limited it. There seemed little possibility of building a house-to-house campaign organization during that period, nor did the budget allow it. "A precinct worker costs $20.00 a day," as one leader said. (Even so, he felt a $10,000 investment might make a difference.) The League ladies did make thousands of telephone calls, and thousands of leaflets were mailed by their efforts. In general, however, little face-to-face persuasion of the voter was attempted.

Instead, personal confrontation ordinarily took the form of speeches made before organized groups. These ranged from PTA to union local, from Unitarian Churches to Rotary meetings. Altogether, some dozens of speakers were busy giving sixty or seventy speeches a week during the eight weeks of the campaign. Their speeches were sometimes single presentations; more often, they were in the Lincoln-Douglas format—a member of the opposition would appear to debate with the campaigner for the District Plan.

Such speechmaking was frequently carried in the newspapers, creating another dimension—propaganda by reflection. Meanwhile, the local educational television station which had televised meetings of the Board of Freeholders also carried a series of debates on the District Plan in the program called "Metroplex." A part of the Ford Foundation's pilot experiment in adult education in St. Louis, the format of the television programs was also bipartisan, with an emphasis upon the pros *and* the cons. Taking its definitions of the issues from the usually uninformed citizens, it is described rather bitterly by a protagonist of the plan.

That program proceeded on the basis of presenting both sides, of finding out what were the issues. The issues they came up with were "taxes" and "an additional layer of government." Now, really, there were other issues—such as traffic, planning, zoning, economic development. They slanted the discussion and I think we really lost through this "educational" program.

Perhaps the most important single channel of information and influence was the coverage of the campaign by the daily papers. Both the *Post-Dispatch* and the *Globe-Democrat* had given wide coverage to the "metropolitan issue" from the days of the Metropolitan St. Louis survey; both took a loud pro-District Plan position. During the last fifteen days of the campaign, each paper carried stories on all but one day. The *Post* carried 39 stories, for an average of almost 60 column inches a day on the Plan; the *Globe* carried 47 stories and an average of nearly 50 inches a day. As the following tables indicate, each of them spent a great deal of editorial space on the issue.

Table 4-1. News Coverage of the District Plan Campaign*

	Post-Dispatch		Globe-Democrat	
	Number of Stories	Inches	Number of Stories	Inches
Editorial	11	125½	6	68
Major News Story	16	421½	19	316¾
Minor News Story	0	0	14	61¼
Letters to Editor	5	28¼	6	54¾
Feature	5	197½	2	185
Cartoons	2	53¼	0	0
	39	826	47	685¾

* October 17 through November 3, 1959.

The reader of the St. Louis metropolitan daily press was in no danger of remaining ignorant, if he cared to find out about the District Plan. These news stories were overwhelmingly in favor of the District

Plan. They either supported it editorially or reported, favorably, on those who had taken public positions for the plan. Thus, the line-up was as follows in the *Post*.

Table 4-2. Distribution of Column Inches Pro and Con the District Plan, Post-Dispatch*

Type of Story	Pro		Con	
	Number	Inches	Number	Inches
Editorial	11	125½	0	0
News Story	16	325½	11	97
Features	4	164	1	33½
	31	615	12	130½

* One story primarily in opposition included 9½ inches of supporting material; 11 stories primarily supportive included 82 inches of the opposition's story.

The columns of the *Post* reported on the positions of 100 organizations or individuals. The division was about two to one in favor of the plan.

Table 4-3. Organizations and Officials by Position on the District Plan

Official Position	Pro	Con
Elected Political, County	3	2
Elected Political, City	10	7
Other Political, City and County	8	8
Other Organizational Leader, City and County	44	18
	65	35

It is clear, on closer inspection, that the preponderance of pro-stories is due almost entirely to the large proportion of *nonpolitical* organization leaders who came out in favor of the District Plan.

In summary, the strategy of the District Plan campaigners was to (hopefully) neutralize the party process. In this truce, it was their aim to dominate the mass media with favorable images of the plan, from editorial support in the papers to testimonials by civic notables. Speeches were to spread the details of the plan through organizational meetings and luncheons. Information and influence were to be, hopefully, spread through a massive telephone campaign and the mailing of many leaflets. The mirrors of the media were to cast back to the public the image of widespread and respectable support for the plan.

The Arguments Used. The specific arguments used invoked the norms of economic progress, improved services, improved order, and equity and cooperation. In short, they rested upon the morality plays of fertility and improved mechanical progress.

Economic progress was the most important argument reflected in the mass media campaign: this from the *Post-Dispatch* editorial page.[3]

We cannot afford to lose time in the 1960's coping with antiquated, overlapping, conflicting local government as we have been forced to do in the 1940's and 1950's. The next urgent steps in metropolitan progress are to broaden the community's economic base and to provide adequate political tools for tackling areawide metropolitan problems . . . For progress—far *greater* progress—vote FOR the District Plan!" [3]

Other headlines ran: "District Plan Called Way to Lighten Tax Load on Homes," "Proposal Called Way to Attract Industry," "Proposal Called 'Means of Insuring Pay Envelope and Cutting Local Tax,'" and so forth.

The second most important argument appearing in the newspapers was that for improved transport in the metropolis. Cartoons depicted the difficulties of rush hour traffic, and the *Globe* carried a story on the plan which moved in this direction:

Today, Metropolitan St. Louis is faced with traffic and transportation problems that will become more acute and demanding unless steps are taken right now to meet them.

Congestion, lack of off-street parking, inadequate roads, increased costs

[3] Editorial, *St. Louis Post-Dispatch*, October 18, 1959.

for transporting goods locally, skyrocketing auto insurance rates for St. Louis car owners—all result from lack of co-ordinated planning and fragmented government.

Other arguments emphasized areawide planning, civil defense, improved cooperation, and equity among the governments. In general, however, fertility and improved transportation were the "kickers." Even the enemies of the plan agreed that the traffic issue was a good one (and it will be remembered that Cervantes' original interest in metropolitan government went back to the areawide traffic problems).

A rather minor aspect of the plan was that calling for areawide coordination of certain police tasks—training, detection laboratories, records, and the like. This item, however, appeared fairly frequently in the newspaper campaign: A DISTRICT FOR GROWTH: TOOLS FOR POLICE TEAMWORK: DISTRICT PLAN CALLED AN AID TO AREAWIDE FIGHT ON CRIME: DISTRICT PLAN HELPS POLICE FIGHT CRIME. The publisher of the *Globe* put it this way, in a television appearance:

> The shocking growth of crime in both city and county makes it absolutely indispensable to good government and to the safety of our families and of the community that we have a better crime prevention and detection system than we have now. . . .
>
> We cannot hope to have it until we take at least this first step toward working together.

Though the crime prevention aspect of metropolitan government may have seemed minor to those who drafted the plan, there is some evidence that it had box office appeal to readers and writers.

The major arguments given in favor of the plan, as they appeared in the *Post* during the last two weeks of campaigning, were as follows (See Table 4-4.)
The campaign, as reflected in the very complete coverage of the major daily, was obviously an honest one. Emphasis was not upon economy, nor was it upon efficiency in the narrow sense. Instead, the headlines were given to fertility and increased services through increased governmental power. Sixty per cent of the arguments fall in the latter category, 24 per cent are based upon increased fertility—only a smattering

Table 4-4. Arguments Made for the District Plan in Post-Dispatch

Argument	Number of Appearances	Percentage
1. Improved economic growth	34	24
2. Improved transportation	26	18
3. Improved land-use, planning	21	14
4. Improved police, civil defense	16	11
5. Improved cooperation, equity	11	8
6. Increased efficiency, lower costs	7	5
7. Industrial development agency (for industrial parks)	6	5
8. Scattered service improvements	17	12
9. All other	5	4
	143	101

refer to the greater coordination, equity, and economy of the new government.

The Hustings. Such a campaign assumes a high level of rationality and understanding among the citizens. At the hustings, the fighting ideology was somewhat different. Bill James, Chairman of the Committee for City-County Partnership, was described as "very effective. He has a fundamentalist pitch that gets them. He's a car salesman, fresh, effective and appealing." James also changed his focus as he spoke to different groups.

He'll give examples of location decisions—very specific cases, like the General Motors branch that wanted to locate here and found that the only available land would provoke a big political hassle. They went elsewhere. Another argument he uses is traffic—he'll tell you how many municipalities you go through on Big Bend in getting from the city to Kirkwood, and how many different speed laws, kinds of signs, kinds of police forces, and so on. When his opponents say, 'It'll cost you money over and above existing taxes,' his answer is, 'We'll get more economic development and more than your fifty cents will be picked up by new industry.'

A more incisive, though also accurate, picture of James at work is presented by an opponent who represented the county municipalities.

He gets up and he says, 'Look, I'm a nice guy. I've got a little school out in the county for a hundred and forty boys—that's Missouri Boy's Town— boys of all kinds. I have a family too. I'm for kids, for their health and schools and parks and playgrounds.' They identify him as a nice guy.

Then he builds up the prestige of the survey—emphasizes all the money and all the professors. Then he says the Board of Freeholders voted for just what was recommended. Then he spends, at most, two minutes on the plan itself.

As the campaign progressed, the emphasis changed somewhat. The carrots remained substantially the same. The answer to the cry of "higher taxes" (that is, economic development) became ever more important. Another theme was added in the county. As a county campaigner put it—"Our PR advice is to emphasize, first, that the district neutralizes the threat of all-out merger." This was to bring the anti-mergerites into line with the District Plan. Another increasingly important argument, reported by an opponent, went as follows:

Look, the proponents of this thing always say, 'This is your last chance. This is the way to progress!' Yet look—how are you going to amend it? . . . Then they'll talk about the people. Everything always goes back to the people.

The assumption behind this argument was that strong pro-mergerites could be brought into line with the District Plan through its suasion.

One of the few campaigners who spent time systematically at precinct level campaigning described his work this way.

I usually have eight or twelve people from a block, who're interested. It's usually a very brief speech and a lot of questions and answers. We get definite results. I feel the personal, direct sale is the best. I don't think you get good results with large audiences. (Why?) I think that the opportunity to ask questions is *very* important to people when you're selling them the plan. Many people, you know, think this is *merger*. When I first started I took it for granted that people knew it isn't a merger plan, but there is widespread ignorance and distrust around, and I no longer assume that.

Oh, I wish we had three more weeks. I don't care what you say and what Bill James says, people are thinking that, 'Whatever happens, whatever arguments we hear, it's still true. We will elect them and they will merge us.'

The proponents' answer to this was, of course, that not one municipality in the metropolis would be abolished by the District Plan.

Thus the campaign progressed, from September through October. In the middle of the campaign, a large "tea party" was given for the District Plan "workers." Professional entertainers appeared (free) and sang a new version of the *St. Louis Blues*.

> I hate to see that shadow on the wall,
> Cause that's a sign the thugs have come to call,
> I'll be scared tomorrow just like I'm scared today,
> Unless we pass the plan and run those hoods away;
> Got the St. Louis Blues, unless we pass that plan,
> Got to get out and win it anyway we can.

(Other verses dealt with hating to see that evening traffic jam, etc.). The Khorassan Room of the city's prestige hotel, the Chase, was the scene of this festive affair—and though the crowd was probably not 2500 and did not overflow the ballroom (as the *Globe* reported), it was a substantial gathering. Furs were in evidence, as were chauffeured cars and sports cars. One of the campaign leaders indicated his response:

Frankly, we were disappointed. We wanted them out in the streets—we were prepared for it—and it didn't come off. We sent out 20,000 invitations. But it wasn't a bad meeting.

Question: Were those workers for the District Plan (as the papers reported).

No; of course we don't have workers like *that*.

The Opposition

The opposition campaign began only after the District Plan protagonists had left the starting line. Like the latter campaign, it was the property of a small and specific group of people. Like the proponents, they were a far from random sample of the metropolitan community. They were, however, much more divided than the pro-District Plan campaigners. There were two formal campaign organizations of some importance, the Citizen's Committee for Self Government and the Citizens against the District Plan.

The first was a wholly suburban movement. It incorporated elected municipal officials of various suburbs, municipal attorneys (who do a lucrative business, sometimes servicing a half dozen municipalities), and the local community press. The city group, Citizens against the District Plan, was financed by local labor unions (the Central Labor Council and the Teamsters) and headed by Holloran, Democratic National Committeeman from Missouri, Hocker, Republican gubernatorial candidate in 1956, and Clark, president of the AFL-CIO Central Labor Council. The unions had always opposed any plan other than merger; they financed the Citizens' group and invited other opponents. Hocker (and probably Holloran) opposed it not only because he preferred merger, but also, as he candidly put it, because he felt as a public figure intending to remain a public figure he had to appear in the campaign in some position.

Between these two campaign groups there was very little communication. The president of the Citizen's Committee for Self Government had not met some members of the other group and did not even recognize the name of their public relations firm (the major PR firm in the St. Louis area). Each group emerged independently, with diametrically opposite criticisms of the plan: the suburban group opposed it because it meant loss of local identity and "merger" with the city. The central city group opposed it because it was far too "weak" and would distract people from the real solution, merger.

The suburban coalition was formed by men who were adamantly opposed to any kind of formal integration with the City of St. Louis.

Local politicians, office-holders, attorneys, journalists, they saw nothing but danger in expanded areawide jurisdictions for government. In the early stages of the campaign, a group of like-minded actors was called together and given a series of arguments against the plan. An effort was made by the president of the committee to raise funds—he could never get over $100 in any single donation, and the final budget was around $2,000. Volunteer help manned a speaker's bureau, a news release office, and the hustings. Labor was donated to print flyers, and the community press of suburbia gave the group a great deal of free space. In addition to their usual opposition to the metropolitan dailies, the community press editors were also sensitive to the possibilities that areawide land-use planning and transportation routing might very well downgrade the congested suburban shopping centers upon which they depend. And, entirely aside from realistic issues, the campaign was a superb opportunity for taking a stand identified with "this community" against the "big city"—without being divisive with respect to intra-community politics.[4]

The Campaign Strategy

The opposition campaigns literally "rode in on the shirt tails" of the campaign for the District Plan. Whenever a speaker went out to present the case for the District Plan, he was likely to find another speaker present to argue against him. This was explained by one of the proponents.

Well, most clubs that want programs do want a debate. They're impressed by some of the names in the opposition and figure they ought to be heard. I struck a blow against free speech the other night at the Catholic Men's

---

[4] Cf. Morris Janowitz, *The Community Press in an Urban Setting*. Glencoe: The Free Press, 1949. For a discussion of the importance of the press in local political processes see Scott Greer; "The Social Structure and Political Process of Suburbia," *American Sociological Review*, Vol. 25, No. 4, pp. 514–526 and "The Social Structure and Political Process of Suburbia: An Empirical Test," *Rural Sociology*, Vol. 27, No. 4, pp. 438–459.

Club. I'd agreed to speak and then sure enough they asked if I shouldn't
have an opponent. I said very firmly, 'No—fifteen minutes just isn't enough
time for a debate!'

As a consequence of this debating society format, the speechmaking of
the proponents was of doubtful effect. One professional politician
remarked:

> Well, I've been through a lot of campaigns, but this is the weirdest I've
> seen. These goddamned debates go on and on—it's funny. Every outfit
> insists on hearing the pro and the con. Usually, say on a bond issue, they
> want it explained. This time they want it debated!

The opposition was, thus, continually being *invited* to present its position, and in a very effective place—opposite the big guns of the campaigners. They frequently spiked those guns.

Aside from the debates, the opposition also had coverage in the daily
newspapers. Though the metropolitan dailies were committed to the
District Plan, they consistently reported the opposition's activities and
statements. There were sixteen news stories on the District Plan in the
last fifteen days of the campaign. One story began as overtly reporting
hostility and opposition (and included $9\frac{1}{2}$ inches supportive) ; fifteen
stories began as supportive, but included a total of 82 column inches
of unfavorable publicity. Such reportage is probably accounted for by
the professional norms of newsmen and the usual format of reporting.
Nevertheless, it was an effective means of spreading the news of dis-
affection among those interested in the issue.

In a similar fashion, the Citizens against the District Plan were on
television several times during the campaign. The reason was simple;
equal time was proffered because the proponents had been given time
to speak for the plan. And the Metroplex Assembly, as noted earlier,
provided a continuous forum on which the plan could be debated in
terms of "issues" which were nothing but the arguments of the opponents. Thus by speechmaking, press publicity, and television appearances, the Citizen's Committee for City-County Partnership laid the
groundwork for their opponents' propaganda.

The Arguments Used. We have already noted two major arguments used against the plan—it would raise taxes and it would create another level of government in what many held was an "over-governmented" area.

The Woodson Terrace Board of Aldermen has voted unanimously against the Greater St. Louis City-County District Plan.

The board stated in a resolution that the plan would add a new unit of government and taxes without eliminating any existing government units except the Metropolitan Sewer District.

Such arguments were common in both the city and the county campaigns. The suburban-city split, however, showed up in the further arguments against the plan. In the city, the following statement by a former president of the Board of Aldermen is typical:

. . . an increase in the cost of local government can only result in dissatisfaction on the part of the people, and they could never be persuaded to vote for another plan if this one does not prove satisfactory to them.

Underlying this criticism is the continued position of the Citizens against the District Plan, that it does not go far enough towards merger. In the suburbs, however, the additional argument against the plan was the loss of representation—the loss of autonomy to the county towns.

The Richmond Heights City Council this week went on record to oppose the Greater St. Louis City-County District Plan.

At its meeting Monday night, the council offered high taxes and control of zoning as reasons for opposing the plan.

As Don Fisher, Dean of the College of Engineering at Washington University and a major opponent, put it:

The property owner who has depended on existing zoning provisions for his protection may suddenly find his own land, or that next door, changed to a new zoning classification. He will also find that a district zoning board will pay little attention to a small group of local citizens who formerly could appear before their own elected city council on such matters.

Thus, beyond their basic agreement that the District Plan would cost more in taxes and would create another level of government, the city and suburban opponents split sharply. The former called the plan too weak; it would not take enough power away from the municipalities: The latter called it too strong; it would take away basic and necessary powers.

Examining the arguments made against the plan as they appeared in the *Post* during the fifteen days of the campaign, they ranked as shown in Table 4-5.

Table 4-5. Arguments against the District Plan Appearing in the Post-Dispatch

Argument	Times Appeared
1. Technical deficiencies	10
2. Cost of government would rise	7
3. Plan too weak	8
4. Plan too strong	2
5. Others	5

In the community press, the arguments against the plan were those discussed, though they had a certain ferocity of tone which was quite different from the staid debates reported in the *Post*. (The *County Observer* reprinted from the *American Mercury* articles in which the Public Administration Service and International City Managers' Association were alleged to be "communist fronts".) Their attacks were extremely simplified, as in this statement from the *St. Louis County Observer*.

Whatever 'metropolitan problems' exist or may arise as anyone well knows are of a peculiarly local nature. That holds true whether they are in the city, in the county or in any one of the county's incorporated areas. Local governments we strongly believe are best able to cope with them and we see no need whatever to set up a district layer of government to do the job.[5]

[5] September 9, 1959, as quoted in *Reform in St. Louis, op. cit.,* page 41.

As their position was turned into a fighting ideology, the suburban opponents relied on an old morality play: the fear of government. Whether they opposed the District Plan as "big government, far from the people," or as simply "more government," requiring more taxes, they relied upon the definition of government against the people and evoked the norms of governmental restraint. The city opponents, however, evoked the morality of increased governmental integration, power, and hence efficiency. By both sets of norms, the District Plan was suspect, a compromise satisfying none.

Nonorganization Opponents. There are two important types of actor which were unaffiliated with either of these *ad hoc* organizations, though perhaps more important than both together. One was the handful of Negro politicians who "count" in the City of St. Louis. The other was a set of political notables of great visibility who had to take a stand, and who opposed the District Plan.

The Mayor of St. Louis, though he made only four speeches against the District Plan, made a series of interlocking criticisms. The plan (1) would not eliminate any existing government, (2) would promote further governmental fragmentation, (3) would not allow consideration of areawide problems such as health and hospitals, (4) would make further extension of the metropolitan district's functions difficult, (5) would not create equitable tax levy and assessments, and (6) would not allow fair representation on the proposed Board of Supervisors.

Though Mr. Tucker was criticized for his position, and second-guessed by opponents and proponents alike, it seems most sensible to follow the lead of one of the wheel-horses of the campaign for the plan.

Well, I just take him at face value. He really wanted another approach, and a lot of arguments are just makeweight. But what hurts is the argument that it wouldn't work—and the hell of it is that it *won't* if nobody believes in it.

Mr. Tucker said, in effect, that the district would not solve any of the city's problems: that in return for giving up trading cards, the city would remain with the same problems it had always faced. A similar position is discernible in all those identified with the city in its political fate and therefore opposed to the District Plan. The county supervisor, McNary, also came out against the plan. His reasons are obscure, but it is clear that he spent some time gauging the probable success of the plan and then went in the same direction as his voters did. He also stated that, as a public figure, he had to take a position on any issue this large—and a position for the interests of the county.

The Negro leaders in St. Louis were not seriously approached by the Citizen's Committee for City-County Partnership, or by their opponents. One Negro leader who had favored the Plan did call a meeting, where he attempted to gain their support. He found, to his dismay, that an overwhelming majority were opposed. Their reasons were several. First, they feared they would not be equitably represented in the district government. (He felt that much of this was a carryover from the battle for a charter in 1957—which Negroes had opposed because it seemed likely to cut down their representation in the Board of Aldermen.) Finally, and perhaps most important, our informant indicated that the Negroes in St. Louis had decided to take a united stand on major community issues and *not to support anything they had had nothing to do with formulating*. This meeting on the District Plan was said to have been the first caucus of Negro political leaders in the history of St. Louis. Perhaps the District Plan campaign was an important catalytic process in the development of Negro politics. But the Negro leaders (and the Negro wards) did not support the plan.

Second-Guessing the District Plan Campaign

Because the metropolitan district plan was a radical innovation, it did not fit neatly into the folk political science of the interested actors. Everybody was forced to either (1) rely upon authority or (2) try to decide for himself, as best he could, what the new government would be like if it ever came about and how it would affect the things that mattered most to him. This meant that one had to translate the provisions of a charter into an image of a flesh-and-blood government, with officials, powers, jails, taxes, policies, politics, and presumably a certain amount of pelf. Such an exercise will tax the most astute practicing political artist: it will allow anybody to drift into a never-never land of hypotheses and assumptions built on assumptions.

Here are some private thoughts of local actors concerning key elements of the District Plan. We have concentrated upon three: (1) its governance, (2) its taxing powers, and (3) its powers relative to the continuing municipalities, county, and other governmental entities.

Governance. The district would have been governed by a council elected by new electoral boroughs and a president elected at large. Here is the way one political inside dopester, a county politician recently out of office, described the consequences as he saw them.

The partisan nature of the district government is objectionable to many people, particularly to the mayors and officials of the county municipalities. A Republican can't be for it because of the political consequences that will flow from the way the boroughs are defined. No matter what happens, of course, the Democrats will be in anyway. (laughs) However, under the non-partisan label we'll get Democrats in whom we don't oppose so much. Partisan or non-partisan they're going to be Democrats. But look here . . . .

(Gets out a map of the official charter and shows the electoral consequences of the boroughs.)

Look, the person who controls the 11th is McAteer, a saloon keeper. The 10th is Sestric, the 9th, Kinney, a State Senator, the 8th, Jordan Chambers, a Negro constable. The 7th, Jellyroll Hogan, the 5th, well, that's Midge Berra on Dago Hill. You see, each of these persons is not just a Democrat but the lowest kind of a Democratic hack politician. They can control the primary and controlling the primary is the equivalent of controlling the election.

Now look where you do run into the county. What you do is run a machine controlled district into the county around Brentwood and there's where you're getting real opposition—in Brentwood. The primary is all that's necessary for control and all the Republicans in Brentwood would have to cross over in the primary in order to have any effect on the election of the representative to the District.

Look at this borough six—you have all of the do-gooders, Clayton, University City, Ladue—all of the do-gooders in one borough. Can't you just see him—a lone voice in this borough council? (laughs) Well, there are seven of your committeemen; all you got to have now is a couple more to control it. Then you've got Bob Young, committeeman in the Airport Township, the steamfitters' union man, a Democrat. You've now got seven of the fifteen controlled by the machine element of the Democratic party. And it would be very easy then to carry someone from the basic anti-Negro areas, they'd come along or one of the four people elected at large would, and you'd have city Democratic machine pols in charge of the district government. This means that, no matter what you do when you begin, you start out with a government controlled by bums!

Another second-guesser emphasized what the plan did to local representation.

The boroughs are too big, too far from the people. They've got no governmental powers either. Maybe it wouldn't be so bad if they had some governmental powers—but mind you I'm not saying that any change at all is necessarily needed.

Others criticized the plan because it gave too much power to the executive, allowed him to appoint too many important administrators. But an opposite point of view was also expressed, by one suburban lawyer who subscribes to National Municipal League principles.

Take the Metropolitan Sewer District. They say you'll have an elected official responsible to the people running it. Why the hell should you? It's a professional job; it will be, after all, a professional job. It should be.

Taxes. The official position of the campaigners for the plan was that it allowed but did not require tax increases. They attempted to underline the public responsibility of those who made the increases and to minimize the total tax burden. The critics indicated that the taxes would be major indeed.

People don't talk about the fact that the sewer district at this moment only has the Mississippi watershed. The rest flows into the Merrimac and the Missouri. If they take the balance of the county into the sewer district it will cost an awful lot of money and this money can only be raised through special tax assessment, special tax districts for sewer purposes. They tell the people it's not going to cost money and it certainly will. Then there'll be ten or fifteen years of litigation before you can possibly get what you need.

Another argument raised the question to another plane.

The city-county fight is antagonistic primarily because of taxes except for the radicals who make it a race war, and the basic conflict can only be solved by a new government which will take the powers of government out of the hands of the machine politicians. The survey's report had a basic organic weakness—you cannot solve the city's problems or the county's problems without the cooperation of the state legislators.

Many disputants spoke of the fiscal weakness of the new district.

"It's far too weak, and the constitutional limits on bonding (5 per cent) are very inadequate. Kerr, who runs the Metropolitan Sewer District, and Kaiser his attorney, are really worried over adequate financing for their operation when they get absorbed in the district."

Others, however, including the County League of Municipalities, spoke as if the district could exceed the constitutional limit, could borrow for any purpose, and could pass special tax bills without hearings. Another amateur political scientist of local government put it this way.

Now as for public ownership of the transit, that's simply out of the question. The tax consequences here are something that are going to be obvious to a lot of people and it's going to hurt in the referendum. People still remember the traffic district referendum. Their $15,000,000 a year won't buy sewers, much less public transit.

Special benefit assessments will have to be done and I'll tell you those special benefit assessments on sewers are already scaring people to death. In the north and west and south county people are up in arms.

The Mayor of St. Louis and the ex-President of the Board of Aldermen emphasized the extra burden to St. Louis taxpayers.

The proposed metropolitan District Plan would not relieve the city of St. Louis totally of any existing function except civil defense. . . . As a result of the duplication of functions . . . the city would certainly not be able to reduce its tax rate by the amount of the new tax rate levied by the proposed Metropolitan District (Tucker).

But a county lawyer emphasized the cost to the growing and prosperous county of the declining central city.

The *Post-Dispatch* is one of those pushing the District. They're worried and their big advertisers are worried about the decline of downtown, and also about the tremendous colored problem. They wanted to bail the city out, through joining up the city and the county!"

Considering how this might come about, another voice intrudes:

The district can levy and collect special assessments for the construction and improvement of public works. . . . This means the individual property owners may be called upon to pay huge sums for a superhighway or a street widening or an expressway, either in front of his property or in the neighborhood thereof (Fischer, *Post-Dispatch*, October 23, 1959).

Then those who are in favor of increasing taxes speak up in these terms:

Its authority to tax real estate is limited to 50 cents per $100 assessed—a maximum of $25 per year for the owners of a $15,000 home. Like any municipal government it can also obtain revenue by special assessments against property benefitted by public improvements. It can issue bonds: but except for bonds for revenue-producing projects to be repaid out of revenues, it can do this only with popular approval registered in a referendum (Eliot, *Post-Dispatch*, October 25, 1959).

Or, as one opponent summed it up,

The opponents also have been very stupid. In my book they say another layer of government—that's bad; they say there'll be more taxes; that's bad—*Of course—we've got to have more taxes.* The proponents and the opponents both make no sense.

Powers of Government. A key bone of contention, as we have seen, was the extent of powers granted to the new district. City critics, headed by the mayor, considered it far too weak. ("Too much has been claimed for the District Plan, and the plan itself is too weak and too doubtful an instrument for carrying out the tasks assigned to it," as Mayor Tucker said on television, October 3, 1959.) Suburban critics saw it as far too strong for their taste. One eccentric galloped around the suburbs dressed up like a Minuteman, indicating, presumably, that the British were coming back. "We should not sell short the ability of the people of the County to solve their problems without being hamstrung by the city".

What were the extent of these powers as seen by local kibitzers? One opponent spoke in this fashion:

The plan . . . includes the power to control practically all streets . . . establish its own police force . . . establish its own courts . . . (collect) a tax to the district about equal to their present city tax . . . control all police and fire departments in the district (in case of emergency) . . . take land away under condemnation proceedings . . . etc., etc. (Fischer, *Post-Dispatch*, October 23, 1959).

Others, however, felt it would have limited and largely obscure powers.

Planning and zoning is going to be a delightful field of litigation. I think they'll have to have another referendum in order to get the power which is not clearly given by this charter. It is now based only on the police power. And zoning in the municipalities can easily be interpreted as directly conflicting with the planning function of the district. You've got a hassle of planning commissioners all over, you've got the County plan, you've got the municipal plans, now you've got a District plan.

Another pointed out problems of language.

The Survey Report wasn't written as a constitution but look, here are phrases coming right from your Report requiring substantial compliance of local zoning with district wide planning. What in the world is 'substantial compliance?' It will take ten years to find out.

Another critic (this time a journalist) noted:

You've got all kinds of conflicts—the police powers of the district and municipality are 'concurrent' in one place, separate in another—look at the litigation you'd get. And powers other than the sewerage district's existing ones are optional to the governing board in one part of the Charter, but in another place it says they're mandatory. There's no provision for initiative, or referendum, or recall.

The only thing that's effective in this plan is the traffic control. It's something people can see and feel every day, and they're real concerned.

But even this was subject to a barrage of criticism.

Yes, the traffic provision is the strongest in the plan. After all, this is something that needs to be handled. And the politicos aren't going to worry about the loss of traffic control. What worries them, though, is the ambiguity. They simply don't know what they'll be expected to do. They don't know what 'approaches to arterials' are. They don't know what they must police and what they cannot police. This will also require a lot of legal work.

On the other hand, those who were campaigning for the Plan had to try, continually, to show that it had adequate powers but not too much power. This was the job taken on by the daily newspapers, who spent column after column on the topic. As Thomas H. Eliot wrote on the editorial page of the *Post*:

The district approach was chosen because it meets the need, no more and no less. It provides a metropolitan government with enough authority to handle metropolitan matters. It confines that government to such matters. It grants power where power is needed. . . . It keeps authority to handle non-metropolitan matters in the hands of the local governments (*Post-Dispatch*, October 25, 1959).

But as one of the more violent opponents of the District Plan from the suburbs remarked:

The strangest thing is that in the city you run into people who say it's no good because it won't produce merger—and in the County they say it's bad because it will produce merger. And the funny thing is that each side is absolutely convinced and you can't argue with them. Personally, I'm sure it will produce merger...

Second-Guessing the Campaign. Throughout the last heated month of the campaign there was a curious lack of certainty as to what was going on. A referendum campaign on a metropolitan government is not an ordinary part of "politics as usual;" it bypasses ordinary mechanisms and disrupts ordinary political alliances. Nor does it fit within the folk technology of politics, as used by the practicing politicians. Literally nobody knows how such a campaign works, and therefore nobody knows how it should be run.

There is not even certainty as to why principal actors are acting. The air is filled with accusations of personal interest, yet those fighting for the District Plan tended to discount personal advantage.

The payoff? There's always a pay-off. Who'd you see in our opposition? (names) Yeah, I've debated with him. I'll tell you his pay-off. First, he just don't like the plan. But look—he's a lawyer and this is going to get him known. It'll help his practice—appearing in public and in print, day after day. (Will it help political careers?) Sure, sure. They'll get a pay-off. There's a pay-off for everybody connected with this campaign, for and against.

But one of this man's allies questioned the statement. "Yeah," wryly, "there's a pay-off. Tell that to my wife." He went on to talk of an official job endangered because of his participation in the campaign. He then spoke of the advantage, for a practical politician, of having Civic Progress, the newspapers, and all the big money on your side. "This campaign is being run by lawyers. This town would fall apart without them—and young lawyers, guys under forty."

This man was described by an opponent. "He's a very ambitious guy, though, who'd do a lot to get on. I think he's simply decided to use this thing. As for Cervantes, he's out to be *Governor!*" Such accusations were rife. Two of the proponents of the District Plan were described by a friendly critic in this fashion.

I'll tell you about him. He wants to be *Governor.* Of course the campaign won't hurt him—he wouldn't do anything that would hurt him. He's a guy who has really hurt the development of planning in the county, and in

———he's been one of the persons who, as an attorney, has fought hardest to disrupt both city and county plans—fighting for zoning waivers, spot-zoning, and the like. The District Plan is being sold and fought under false pretenses.

Another protagonist indicated he went along for the public interest: "there's nothing in it for a practicing lawyer." For his opponents, however, he adduced these reasons: "Well, in the first place, the politicians want to be on the winning side, the bandwagon. Second, many of these petty politicians feel that their vested interest is threatened by the plan." When this was discussed with others, they noted that this man had been a major and effective opponent of county reorganization, while Cervantes, head of the district plan committee, had fought the new charter for the City of St. Louis (1957) tooth and nail.

Underlying much of the reasoning of the protagonists was something which can only be called "local patriotism." As one leader put it:

This is a good town, I love this town, but it's dying. I've felt it you know— I lived there until I was four, in the city, and I have a strong feeling for the city. When my kids are grown up I'll move right back to the river front. The west end's o.k., but I want to sit there and watch that old river roll on.

And Cervantes said: "Ever since I have been old enough to listen, I have heard people saying that the St. Louis area is in a rut, that something should be done to kick it awake. Here, now, is the chance to do that something" (*Globe,* October 25, 1959).

The leaders of the campaign for the plan, like any political leaders, were undoubtedly aware of both the career possibilities and dangers of the commitment. They were also involved in the substantive program; how much so is difficult to determine. And as the campaign went on, they probably became more involved—the mere process of working for a goal tends to result in increased commitment. Those who were opposed were also, in some cases, committed to a staunch rejection of the plan on its face. Others were public officials who had to take a stand because of reputational position. Of these, many saw a political pay-off in defeating the plan—"He's going to take credit for killing it," as one observer remarked of a leading opponent.

The dozens of young lawyers who went on the hustings deserve a brief comment of their own. For them, the campaign for the plan (and against it) allowed them access to the media. If they had claims of political influence in a given locale, it made possible a testing of that influence at the public expense—a free survey of the voters. Finally, as a young suburban lawyer who was involved summed it up:

Well, you know———hasn't done anything in politics since 1954—except a lot of good works of one kind and another. You know a lot of lawyers have a lot of free time—and they look for things to do.———is in that position now, and says so frankly. He's out of a job and doesn't want to rebuild a law practice.

Nobody was certain as to the commitment of the proponents or the opponents. Nor was anybody certain as to how the campaign should be run. Estimates of the money needed ranged from the $70,000 or so collected to a quarter of a million. Nor did anybody know what the involvement of different figures meant. Tucker's position was generally regarded as harmful to the plan—though others remarked that it might hurt Tucker with his supporters, the press and the businessmen and the good government people. Some thought Tucker's opposition neutralized the opposition of the city ward organizations, old enemies of Tucker. In brief, nobody was certain.

One opinionated person sketched out a critique:

These people should have tiptoed in. What they have done is go around and get people involved who would rather have sat it out by asking them 'Which side are you on?' Once they've said they're against it and you've blasted them in the paper, then they have an investment, by golly, and then they're going to get into the campaign with a vengeance.

This criticism, however, ignores the entire logic of the campaign, which required that a long series of notables and civic leaders should appear in the mass media endorsing the campaign.

And indeed, the list is long. Heads of Civic Progress, the local Universities, the Chamber of Commerce, such major industries as Southwestern Bell, the McDonnell Aircraft Company, and the major banks did go on record. (These included the top echelons of the "power struc-

ture" as described by local informants who believed they were knowledgeable.) Some of their statements were as closely reasoned and impressive as that of Mayor Tucker. Yet when the critic quoted above
was asked about the endorsement of the charter by the Big Mules, he
laughed and said: "They haven't read it." And evidence indicates that
many had not. They were used to delegating their political judgment to
Tucker: when it developed that they had misunderstood him, they back-
tracked rapidly.

The Citizen's Committee for the Plan was also criticized for ignoring
the Negroes. They had not made an effective impression on the
N.A.A.C.P., and they avoided the Negro political leaders. On the other
hand, their strategy may have been a wise one. This is how a leader
described it.

"The Negroes took a stand—negative."

Question: "Leaders or people?"

"Leaders."

Question: "Will this have an effect?"

"No, and I'll tell you why. Negro voters don't get in if it isn't a race issue.
We've been absolutely quiet on this, and haven't approached the Negro
wards—no leaflets, no nothing. They don't read the paper and so they won't
vote, one way or the other. If we put out a leaflet, next thing you know they
hear their big leader is against it and they might vote."

In fact, however, the District Plan took its worst beating in St. Louis in
a Negro ward whose leader had fought against it.

Though the campaign was predicated on the mass media, many felt
that a widespread block campaign would have been more effective.
Others, however, believed that the election went completely outside
the range of media persuasion. One opponent interpreted it this way.

No man can carry over two hundred votes on this thing. I can't. Tucker
can't. Jimmie here can't. That's all. I can carry as many as Tucker. And
that's the way it is. Local politics works on the pyramid system—you get
these little blocks together and build your pyramid. The other side is depending on the newspapers, on money, on television, on big names. We're going
to use the pyramid system.

On the other hand, the proponents did not subscribe to this belief at all. "Tucker's hurt us bad, there's no doubt about it. He's killing us on the South Side—and he has a half dozen wards there."

As for the probable results of the campaign, few people were optimistic, yet few would commit themselves to an estimate of either turnout or proportion pro and con. The opponents were especially chary. "It's a horse race;" "It'll be a huge turnout;" "The pros will turn out and the opponents will stay home;" and one suburban leader even said, "I thought until the election they'd win. I actually bet a drink the District Plan would pass. (Why?) Because the papers were campaigning so strongly for it. They were brainwashing the people."

In the camp of the proponents, however, gloom had descended by the last week of October.

Well, it looks bad. The crowds at the meetings are not having any, and some of them are downright hostile. . . . It's losing. Of course we try not to look defeated in public.

I really don't know what the turnout will be. I shouldn't say this, but a lot of us have recently hoped we'd have a small turnout and we could get all of our supporters to feel a certain pessimism. If everybody who cares votes, we stand a decent chance of carrying a small turnout. We're hoping people against the plan will feel they don't need to vote because anyone in his right mind will vote against it.

One of the major leaders put it this way: "I'd feel a lot better as an opponent."

The campaign just didn't catch on. We had two months and they don't understand or know what it's all about. There must have been seventy-five editorials, and the papers average two columns a day on it. I think it really depends on how much they care about something like traffic.

Question: How bad a beating is bad?

Anything worse than three-to-two is bad. But if you come close you really say—"What could we have done differently that would have won?" In a way it's refreshing to get beaten badly. You know you just had a real loser and that's all there is to it.

The proponents of the plan had a much more accurate knowledge of its fate than did the opponents. This seems to be due to their areawide focus (each set of opponents was localized) and to their systematic telephone surveys. Thus they could say, "Right up the middle of the county it's unbelievably good. But in the north and south it's awful. In the Lemay district it's so bad we're afraid even to call. Nobody likes it."

The operational devices used in practical politics are made clear in the following statement. It was made a week before the election by the political sparkplug and major professional on the campaign committee.

It's a loser. It's just not going to make it. Maybe—oh, hell, maybe we could get in on an election like Truman did in 1948, where the 'no's' don't vote and you get a light turnout—we might slip through. But it doesn't look good. I would guess we might lose by 40-60 in the city, maybe 30-70 in the county.

Question: Why do you think so?

Well, first our telephone surveys. They were real good at first, up until a week or so ago. But today we get 138 against, 92 for, and 300 plus don't know. The rest aren't going to vote. (Sample?) We pick 'em at random from a backward phone book.

Then I was talking at St. Louis High, and the kids voted—600 against, 300 for—that's their parents' preference, you know.

Question: Any other reasons?

Look at this campaign headquarters, a week before the election. There ought to be a crowd of people in here milling around, and look—nobody. This campaign never got off the ground. And another thing—the responses in the meetings aren't good. And we have trouble raising money. And volunteers—that too, we can't get 'em. And then, the ward leaders are opposed, and if their people were for it, they'd go along. Nope, it doesn't look good by any sign.

While he was over-optimistic, his prediction was the most precise and accurate made by any political actor interviewed. As we shall see, his "signs" were correct.

Cuyahoga and Dade Counties

Like the metropolitan charters, the campaigns in the other metropolitan areas bear a striking resemblance to that in St. Louis. In each case a mass media campaign was launched, notables were lined up, and the areawide organizations supported the new charter. In Cuyahoga a real effort was made to use the political organizations.

This time every county-wide organization, the suburban mayors' organization, the architects, the Democratic party, the AFL-CIO, everyone endorsed it, and this time they got a real gift of money from the Chamber of Commerce. They really got people to work. They corrected the weaknesses one could see in the 1950 campaign, and yet this campaign did not do as well as the 1950 campaign. I can't second guess the campaign. It wasn't their mistakes.

However, the effort to "use the politicos" did not work well either. The mayor of the central city, Celebrezze, opposed the charter; this in turn led his City Law Department and the heads of administrative agencies to take the leadership of the opposition campaign.

At the same time, it hampered the relationship with the regular Democratic party, which had officially endorsed the charter. In the words of one highly placed official:

When we saw Celebrezze was against it, we said, 'Well then, we'll go to the wards. And I said to the Chamber guys, I said, 'If the men are going to work in the wards, we're going to need some money for them to work with.' And they said, 'Okay.' No question about it.

But, they waited so late in order to get the money to me that I couldn't use it to get people committed. Therefore, I didn't know who to back and who not to, and since the Democratic organization had endorsed it unanimously, we decided to give the money to the organization. Miller, however, felt he could not use party discipline on the matter. So instead he took it and instead of giving it to the people who cared about the charter and were going to fight for it, he divides it up evenly among the Democratic candidates in all 33 wards. Those who were for it, against it, and neutral—all of them got a share!

But as a man less friendly to the Democratic organization put it:

Ray Miller was against the charter all the way. He went out and told his ward men. He said 'Nobody's going to get thrown out of this organization on this issue. There are honest differences of opinion here. If you don't think it's right, you don't have to. Both sides have a perfect right to speak at the Club meetings on the issue.

Well hell, from Ray Miller that's the same thing as saying that he's opposed to the charter. He knifed it.

The coalition in favor of the charter used the same tactics that were used in St. Louis. Lectures were given, speeches and debates were heard, television programs were produced, the newspapers were filled with propaganda, and fliers were mailed. In some wards there was even precinct activity. The opposition, as in St. Louis, used the campaign to fight the charter. They spoke in opposition, and their story was carried as a trailer to the stories favorable to the charter in the daily papers.

The opposition was not large. ("Five men is all it takes to beat a charter I guess," as one embittered proponent remarked. "Because that's all there were.") In addition to the city bureaucrats, there was one important suburban mayor, and equally (if not more) important, the leadership of the Negro political organizations. As in St. Louis, the Negroes were not going to have anything to do with the metropolitan idea: as in St. Louis, they were effective. (Had Negroes in Cleveland voted in 1957 as they did in 1950 the charter would have passed in the city; instead, they opposed by two to one, a complete reversal.)

One statement of the Negro leaders' objections is given here.

In the first place, they have set it up so that the Negroes in the metropolitan council are in an ethnic ghetto; they can elect two and only two representatives. In the second place, that charter would write the protection out of Civil Service, and you know how important Civil Service is to my people. They have a better shake there than in industry. They have better jobs and if you put those jobs into a county government without Civil Service, the chances are that a lot of people will lose their jobs.

A little later in the interview, he became considerably more heated.

But look. These were my arguments in the campaign and I think they're good ones, but I'll tell you what I'm really burned up about. I think that my people have got to be treated with respect. They have got to be respected and that's my program and that's what I'm going to fight for and if I lose I don't care, because they can't hurt me. I tell you they just can't hurt me.

Well, we've just got to make self-respecting citizens out of the Negroes. They've got to behave right but they've got to be treated right. They have got to have good services, they have got to have good political leaders. The city government has got to treat them like everybody else.

We have just got to stop this business of the white people treating us without any respect. Lindseth (leader of the charter campaign) came down to us, to the assembled Negro community political leaders, and he said: 'Gentlemen, what is this going to cost us?'

They got to respect us, we're going to make them respect us. We're going to show them they have got to. *And they better get those handkerchief-heads out of my ward!*[6]

Thus the campaign in Cuyahoga County, although it probably neutralized the political party organization, did not harness it. It was a "good government" coalition, but it did not placate the "minorities"—suburbanites, Negroes, and Republicans. Trouble emerged in each of the three segments of the population. The trouble took the form of vigorous campaigning against the charter at precinct level in the Negro wards and in one suburb. These went overwhelmingly against the charter, in contradistinction to their past performances.

As in St. Louis, the opponents spent great ingenuity criticizing the technical form of the charter. (As a disgruntled proponent remarked, "Anybody can flyspeck a complicated charter.") This criticism, however, was important chiefly when it was reflected in the dailies and the local community press. There was little all-out involvement in the

[6] Some observers point out the relationship between increasing Negro representation in central city government and opposition to Metro. Richard A. Watson and John H. Romani document a decline from 72 per cent "pro" to 29 per cent, as the number of Cleveland Negro councilmen went from 4 to 8 ("Metropolitan Government for Metropolitan Cleveland: An Analysis of the Voting Record," *Midwest Journal of Political Science*, Vol. V, No. 4, pp. 365–398.)

campaign. Of 1,000,000 voters, 40 per cent voted. The audience rating of a television show on the charter was 9—that for Wagon Train (at the same hour) was 40.

Nor was there much competence in respect to the charter and what it held. One ward politician who was committed to the charter said bitterly, "The people just didn't know what it was all about. I've been going around making speeches since the end of the campaign trying to find out why it failed. Most of them didn't even know, for instance, that it wouldn't abolish the different municipalities." The President of the Cleveland City Council, a prototype of the old-style ward politician, said simply, "They were talking over the people's heads."

The charter gained 48 per cent of the votes in the suburbs, 42 per cent in the City of Cleveland.

In Miami, the campaign was also a media campaign. As a co-chairman remarked later, "The press either 'brainwashed the people' or 'did a hell of a job of keeping people informed and educated.'" A mass media executive elaborated: "The *News*, the *Herald*, our TV station, all pounded away at what a good thing it was: 'Give Miami a chance to be a big city' and so forth."

There was very little opposition in Miami. "Who's against home and mother?" as one person put it. Those who did oppose were so poorly organized that they did not even have speakers to engage in debate with the proponents. A number of observers thought that if the opposition had been organized they would have beaten Metro. But the leaders, the media (and as one person added, the brains) were all on one side. Even so, Metro only passed by a few hundred votes.

So much for the prehistory of the campaigns and the way they were seen from the top. We have discussed the organizing of persuasion as organizers viewed it; now it is relevant to look at persuasion as it worked out at the grass roots. Unfortunately we cannot cover all three campaigns adequately, so we turn back to the one for which data are available, the referendum for the Greater St. Louis City-County District Plan.

5

Who Was Listening?

The referendum election for the St. Louis District Plan was held on November 4, 1959. Twenty-one per cent of the registered voters in the City of St. Louis voted, as did 40 per cent of the suburbanites in the county. The plan was overwhelmingly defeated, by two to one in the city (21,450 for, 43,237 against) and by three to one in the county (27,633 for, to 82,738 against). In the history of referenda on such issues in the St. Louis area, this was the most overwhelming defeat ever suffered by the proponents of change.

Immediately after the election, the Center for Metropolitan Studies of Northwestern University carried out a sample survey of the residents. Three hundred and twelve interviews were taken, 116 in the city and 196 in the county.[1] The residents interviewed were those who

[1] The 1957 sample had consisted of 1 per cent of the residences in the suburban county, ¼ per cent of the residences in the central city. The 1959 sample was based upon the residences where there were completed interviews from 1957, since comparisons over time were desired. Wishing to maximize the probability that we were sampling potential *electorate*, we further limited the 1959 sample draw to those who reported in 1957 that they voted in local elections while living in their present area. After the decision to eliminate those who had moved into the sample residence since 1957 from the sample interviewed, we succeeded in interviewing approximately 85 per cent in the county, 75 per cent in the city. The response could have been brought to a higher level through continued interviewer effort; however, the interview depended on rather detailed recall, and because more than a month had already elapsed by the time this level was reached, there was serious question as to the value of further interviews.

lived in the houses where the respondents in the 1957 survey lived. Wherever possible, they were the same respondents; the rate of residential mobility, however, lowered the proportion of identical respondents who could be interviewed. The sample interviewed was, furthermore, a sample of those who had indicated in 1957 that they had voted in local elections. We took this as a fair estimate of the registered voters. Thus the sample was "loaded" for those who would be more politically alert and active and apt to vote in the referendum of 1959.

The survey was designed to continue the study of local political participation begun in 1957. It amounted to a panel study, after the election, on the central topic of the 1957 interviews. However, the amount of residential mobility in American cities is very great, averaging around 10 per cent a year (with a high of 24 per cent in Los Angeles as of 1950). Thus we expected to find that approximately one-third of our respondents had moved in the meantime. Nor were we disappointed: 25 per cent of the houses in our original sample draw were now occupied by other tenants.

From much work of this sort (including the 1957 study) we suspected that the "new arrivals" would be very little concerned with the issues of the referendum.[2] Involvement in local political affairs is closely correlated with length of time in the residence, for this is an indicator of general commitment to a residential area. However, it seemed prudent to test this assumption by interviewing the new arrivals in both city and county. Sixty-six interviews were taken with randomly selected individuals who had moved into their residence since the 1957 survey, 35 in the city and 31 in the county. These interviews do not constitute a representative sample of all the newcomer households, for the results confirmed our prediction that it was wasteful to continue the exercise.

Stated briefly, the newcomers' opinions were similar to others in their neighborhood, but only a relatively tiny proportion were interested, informed, or involved. So unrepresentative and relatively unimportant are these residents, that we shall not discuss them further. Their responses support an important generalization, however: the effective

[2] Cf. Bollens, *op. cit.*, Part 3, "Citizen Participation and Attitudes."

Table 5-1. Interest and Voting in Referendum: Newcomers and Old Residents

	Percentage Who Had:	
	Voted	Heard about the District Plan
City		
Old Resident	30	78
Newcomer	6	60
Suburb		
Old Resident	60	93
Newcomer	26	77

electorate in local affairs is overwhelmingly composed of the "old-timers" in the neighborhoods.

The remainder of this analysis will rest, then, upon the older residents who were interviewed in both 1957 and 1959. They amount to 81 interviewees in the city and 165 in the county. Both because of its size and its relative freedom from bias, the county sample will be the more central focus of inquiry. The response rate was higher, in both surveys, and the "fall-out" from mobility lower in this sample. It represents a response of approximately 85 per cent from a sample of the universe who lived in the same residence in 1959 as in 1957, and who were at least minimally involved in local politics.

How Did They Vote and How Did They Lean?

These two samples, selected to exaggerate the politically alert and active, reveal the massive nature of opposition to the District Plan in

Table 5-2. Percentage Vote, and Preference of Nonvoters, in the Referendum

	Voters			Nonvoters			Total	
	Pro	Refused	Con	Pro	Divided	Con	No Opinion	
City	7	3	20	6	10	13	41	100% (85)
County	14	1	41	6	11	11	16	100% (165)

city and county. Several interesting conclusions may be drawn from Table 5-2. First, if we assume that those who refused were supporters of the plan (and this would seem possible, since it was unpopular and an overwhelming loser), the division of the vote is very close to the overall division in the electorate. Second, there is no evidence that the nonvoters with opinions were very different in their sentiments from the voters. Third, it is clear that the massive opposition in the county was combined, in the city, with massive indifference.

So great is the hostility to the plan, as revealed in these data, that one cannot imagine any kind of turnout that would have changed the results. If all the nonvoters with divided opinions went to the pro column, as they certainly would not be expected to do, the result would have still been a clear defeat in the city and a 5 to 3 defeat in the county. Staying in the realm of common sense, it is likely that any possible increase in turnout would have failed to change the proportions of defeat in any significant degree.

The Campaign and the Communications Network

The campaign for the District Plan covered, at the most generous estimate, the 6 months from the Board of Freeholders' decision to November 4. It was active and noisy, however, only in the last 2 months. During this period, as we have seen, the protagonists sought to fill the airwaves and the press, to load the mail and the telephone wires, and to populate the forums of organizational meetings with their messengers and messages. During the last month, their opponents retaliated in kind: the Citizens against the District Plan, particularly, gained access to the metropolitan media, while the Committee for Self Government mounted the rostrum in debate. Depending now on our sample survey of the citizens, we wish to learn: (1) Who got across the footlights to them? (2) What did they hear? (3) What did they say among themselves?

Turning to the first question, we must recall the organization of the campaign. The chief protagonists were individual leaders, such as Cervantes, Tucker, and Holloran, together with involved organizations—the *Post-Dispatch*, the League of Women Voters, the AFL-CIO Central

Labor Council, and the like. The three *ad hoc* organizations were, essentially, coalitions of organizations and free-floating civic leaders with a reputational stake in the outcome. We will be interested in who was heard and how they got across. That is, what media of communication were important in carrying the messages from leaders to led—the dailies, the organized groups, personal contact, television—or what?

Who Got Across?

We will first analyze the effects (pro and con) of the leadership structure in the metropolitan area and the local communities upon the voters. We used two devices for this purpose: first, we asked the respondents if they knew of any areawide leaders who were for (or against) the District Plan; then, we asked if they knew of any leaders in their own local community who were for (or against) the plan. Second, the respondent was given cards listing the leaders of the three *ad hoc* organizations who had fought for and against the plan, together with constituent organizations and such important nonaffiliates as Mayor Tucker.

Nine per cent of the city respondents could name at least one metropolitan leader who had supported the plan. In the suburbs, the percentage was considerably higher—22 per cent could name an areawide supporter. In all, the 81 city residents named leaders only 10 times, for 5 could name only one leader, one could name 2, and one 3. In the suburbs there were more persons who could name several leaders; twenty-five named one, eight named 2, and two persons named 3—for a total of 47 mentions.

The effectiveness of the areawide leaders must be qualified, however. They got their name across, connected with the general topic, but they did not get their stand on the issue across with much consistency. Of the 47 times suburbanites mentioned areawide leaders supporting the District Plan, they were completely inaccurate 20 times; the city respondents were wrong four out of ten times. In 40 per cent of the cases, those considered to be supporters of the plan by our respondents were on public record as *opposed* to it.

Much of this error is located (if not clarified) when we analyze the public positions of those taken to be leaders for the plan. In the county, more than half the respondents naming a leader thought Tucker was for the plan, and several believed the County Supervisor, McNary, was for it. The error in the city was due to those who believed the Mayor supported the plan. Of those supporters who were named, only Cervantes was named by as many as eight respondents—less than a third of those naming any leader for the plan, and less than 5 per cent of the sample interviewed.

Many more persons responded when asked to name areawide leaders *against* the District Plan. Twenty-six per cent in the city, and 41 per cent in the county could name one such leader. In addition, 6 per cent in the city and 17 per cent in the county named two or more.

Those who named leaders in opposition were accurate in their imputation. This is because of their giving the same names that created error in the imputations of support. Eighty-five per cent of those who could name areawide leaders opposing the plan named Mayor Tucker, in city and in county. A third of the county respondents who named anyone named McNary, as did a fifth in the city. Yet it must be remembered that a strong majority in the county, and an overwhelming one in the city, could not name a single areawide leader in opposition—though the political air had been full of pronouncements for months. Only a third of the sample in the area knew, correctly, where the Mayor of the City of St. Louis stood; only 15 per cent of those in the county knew where the county supervisor stood. And these two figures loomed above any other leaders in the number of folk who imputed positions to them.

When the respondents were asked to name *local* leaders, in their own municipality or section of the city, who had supported the plan, the results were very thin. *Nobody* in the city could name any local leaders supporting it; only 7 per cent of the county sample named even one. Of the 10 persons named, 8 were correctly placed with reference to the issue. Seven were officials in county municipalities—the others were business or professional people.

More persons could name local leaders who were opposed, particularly in the county, but the results still fell short of any show of strength.

Twelve per cent in the county and 6 per cent in the city knew of at least one local opponent. The opponents, again, were correctly designated. Their roles were simply distributed; in the suburbs, they were local municipal officials; in the city, private business and professional people.

Thus, out of all the hullabaloo, very few faces stood out for the crowd. Of those that did, many were surrounded by the wrong halo. The only message that got across clearly to a large proportion of the sample was that Mayor Tucker was opposed. Nor is this strange. When asked what they thought the leaders pro and con had done in the campaign, the respondents gave a few repetitive answers: 'Spoke on television," "made statements for newspapers," or "made speeches" reported in both media. In short, leadership was effective only when reflected (and magnified) by the mass media. The central city mayor is a well-known character in the metropolitan mass media; he is the only actor vying in celebrity with Hollywood figures and comic strip characters. Furthermore, all that he does in public is news. Mayor Tucker might well be called the only leader with a popular following in the St. Louis metropolitan area who affected the referendum of Autumn, 1959.

As noted, a further check was made on awareness of leaders involved in the campaign. Respondents were given a list of the most active, including fifteen leaders, eight who opposed and seven who supported the District Plan. (It also included one "ringer," thrown in as a check on validity of the data.) The leaders who backed the plan included four who were men of stature before the campaign, men whose area of operation was either the central city or the metropolis as a whole. These were: Al Cervantes, President of the Board of Aldermen and head of the campaign in the city; Edwin M. Clark, a key figure in Civic Progress and head of Southwestern Bell Telephone Company; William James, the successful young automobile dealer, known favorably as founder and sponsor of the Missouri Boy's Town, and head of the Citizen's Committee for City-County Partnership; Aloys Kaufman, ex-Mayor of the City of St. Louis (its last Republican mayor) and head of the Metropolitan St. Louis Chamber of Commerce. Three other leaders for the campaign were more parochial in their influence; all centered their efforts in the county. They were: Jackson Daniels, a young lawyer and municipal attorney for a major middle-class suburb, unsuccessful aspirant for office, and early sponsor (with Cervantes) of the Citizen's Committee; Carroll Donahue, another suburban lawyer, active in Democratic politics in the county and head of the campaign in the suburbs; Byron Purteet, a man of good will and the member of the Board of Freeholders responsible for drafting the District Plan.

Of the eight opponents of the plan, five were leaders of some stature. These included: Holloran, Democratic National Committeeman from Missouri and a power in Missouri Democratic politics; Lon Hocker, defeated candidate for the governorship on the Republican ticket in the most recent election; and Joseph Clark, head of the AFL-CIO Central Labor Council. These three (known conventionally as an "unholy alliance") came out together, and late, in opposition to the district plan. They were the peak names of the Citizens against the District Plan. Two others in this category had no open connection with that movement. One was Charles Vatterott, a member of the Board of Freeholders, suburban developer, and Papal Knight—a man completely committed to all-out merger of city and county. The other was Ray Tucker, Mayor of the City of St. Louis. The lesser leaders among the opponents included these: Roy Bergman, suburban lawyer and, with his father, municipal attorney for several suburban communities; Raymond Parker, Mayor of Brentwood, a middle-class suburb; Tillman Hardy, a wealthy eccentric (the man who put on costume and played the role of Minuteman, galloping from suburb to suburb and spreading the news). These three were in the spearhead of the Citizen's Committee for Self Government. Each had a very local, suburban reputation.

We turn first to the simple question: who recognized their names and knew their leadership position and their position on the plan? The results are given in Table 5-3 (leaders who were for the plan) and Table 5-4 (those who opposed). (We have omitted the "ringer"; none of our respondents claimed to recognize the spurious name. This is some support for the validity of the interview.) Of those leaders who pushed the plan to public consciousness, only Cervantes was known as an advocate to as many as 10 per cent in either part of the metropolitan area. Eighteen per cent in the county and 9 per cent in the city knew where he stood. He was also by far the most widely recognized, and one-third of the city residents (who are his consituents, because of his election at large to the position of President of the Board of Aldermen) knew his formal political position. He was more widely known and his position was more widely recognized, however, in the suburbs. None of the other leaders who supported the plan were well enough known for even 10 per cent of the residents to give their correct political or social base of leadership.

Of those who opposed the plan a much larger proportion were well known. Hocker, Holloran, Vatterott, and Tucker, were recognized as "names" by substantial proportions of the residents, ranging from 91 per cent of the suburban residents who recognized Tucker to 25 per cent of the city residents who knew Holloran's name. When, however, we asked if they knew these leaders' position, pro or con, on the district plan, only Hocker and Tucker seemed to have registered accurately with as many as 10 per cent of the residents. Only 12 per cent knew where Hocker stood (in the county, where a Republican has more following) : but 55 per cent in the county and 33 per cent in the city knew where the Mayor of St. Louis stood.

The opponents of the district plan were more representative of the political establishment in the area. It is interesting to note, however, that their positions with respect to the "power structure" were unknown to most of the population. Hocker and Holloran, in fact, were known primarily for their nonpolitical activities. (Vatterott is not a primarily political figure.) Only Tucker was known correctly to a large proportion as a political leader.

It is also important to note how seldom the respondents recognized *any* of the smaller-scale leaders. Daniels, Donahue, and Purteet were of course primarily active in the county. Donahue, however, was a co-chairman of the Citizen's Committee for City-County Partnership, and worked vigorously in speeches and on the media. Nevertheless, even in the suburbs, only 12 per cent recognized his name and *only 2 per cent* knew that he supported the plan. The case was hardly different for the smaller-scale leaders of the opposition: less than 5 per cent of the suburban residents queried knew that any of the three were on record in opposition to the Plan.

Table 5-3. Respondents' Recognition of Leaders for the Plan and on Their Positions: Political and on This Issue (by Percentage)*

Leader Named	Recognized	Gave Position on Plan			Knew Social or Political Position		
	Name	Accurate	Unknown	Inaccurate	Political	Non-Political	Unknown
Cervantes							
City	58	9	46	4	36	1	21
County	62	18	39	5	45	—	17
Ed Clark							
City	1	1	—	—	1	—	—
County	11	3	8	—	7	—	4
James							
City	10	6	4	—	—	6	4
County	18	9	8	1	1	8	9
Kaufman							
City	4	—	4	—	1	—	3
County	26	7	16	3	8	—	18
Daniels							
City	4	—	4	—	1	—	4
County	10	1	8	1	4	—	6
Donahue							
City	5	1	4	—	3	—	2
County	12	2	10	—	3	—	9
Purteet							
City	1	—	1	—	2	—	—
County	5	1	2	2	—	—	5

*Percentages based on 165 cases in county, 81 in city.

Table 54. *Respondents' Recognition of Leaders against the Plan and Their Positions, Political and on This Issue (by Percentage)*

Leader Named	Recognized Name	Gave Position on Plan			Knew Social or Political Position		
		Accurate	Unknown	Inaccurate	Political	Non-Political	Unknown
Holloran							
City	25	2	22	1	6	9	10
County	32	7	21	4	8	14	10
Hocker							
City	39	1	37	1	7	9	10
County	68	12	49	7	13	22	33
Joe Clark							
City	2	—	1	1	—	2	—
County	12	1	10	1	3	—	9
Vatterott							
City	38	1	31	6	1	31	6
County	73	5	50	18	4	56	13
Tucker							
City	75	33	21	21	70	—	5
County	91						
Bergman							
City	6	1	5	—	88	1	2
County	6	—	6	—	2	—	4
Parker							
City	3	—	3	—	1	—	5
County	10	4	5	—	—	—	3
Hardy							
City	5	—	5		6	—	4
County	9	3	6		3	—	7

In summary, it is clear that visibility on such an issue is limited to a very few persons. Tucker, Cervantes, and Hocker (in the county) got their message through to more than 10 per cent of the residents. Tucker towered above all the others as an effective spokesman. However, it is also clear that there is a marked correlation between the recognition of a man's name and knowledge of his position on the plan. And there is a correlation between political (or social) position and recognition. To state it simply, we would hypothesize that (1) certain positions make their incumbents especially visible to the mass media; (2) this, in turn, makes them visible to the citizens; (3) because they are visible (stand on a platform, have a microphone) they can get a message across. On the contrary, no matter how hard a person works, if his position does not give him salience through the media he will not come through. Some of his message may do so, but it will not be associated with him. In short, only at the peak of the *newspapers'* definition of the "power structure" is there any connection between leaders and led.

Organizations Getting Through. The citizens interviewed were handed a card listing ten local organizations involved in the campaign. Four supported the plan, two opposed, and one was neutral. (The neutral organization was introduced as a check on the respondents' knowledge.) In addition, they were asked about the three *ad hoc* organizations put together for the campaign, the Citizen's Committee for City-County Partnership (pro), the Citizens against the District Plan (con—a central city organization), and the Citizen's Committee for Self Government (con—a suburban organization). Of these organizations, 75 per cent in the city and 92 per cent in the county recognized at least one. The median number recognized in the city was three; in the county it was almost six. The difference in familiarity with organizations between city and county held true for every major local organization—suburbanites were more familiar with the organizations involved. The results of this inquiry are presented in Table 5-5.

Several interesting conclusions may be drawn from these findings. First, the three major organizations supporting the District Plan (the *Post-Dispatch*, the League of Women Voters, and the Chamber of

Commerce) were much more effective in making their position understood than were the two opponents of the plan (the County League of
Municipalities and the AFL-CIO Central Labor Council). Second, of
the three *ad hoc* committees only one came through with any volume—
the Citizens against the District Plan. Third, the proportion of the
sample which *correctly* stated the position of any given protagonist was
never as much as half; even the *Post-Dispatch,* with a powerful medium
to place its messages in most of the homes in the metropolitan area,
only reached about one-third of the sample accurately. Three-fourths
did not know where the League of Women Voters stood (though they
worked furiously at the campaign), and 85 per cent had never heard
of the best known *ad hoc* committee in the city. Fourth, the AFL-CIO
Central Labor Council, which voted unanimously to oppose, was
thought (by a large majority of those with opinions) to be in favor
of the District Plan. Fifth, the N.A.A.C.P., with no position on the
plan, had as many persons impute a position to it as did the rabid
(though small) Citizen's Committee for Self-Government. (All imputations were incorrect—it was generally supposed, by those who guessed,
that the N.A.A.C.P. favored the plan.

A final important item should be noted. A higher proportion in the
county recognized the positions of all organizations seriously involved
with the campaign. This is quite consonant with the turnout of voters
in the campaign. The issue appeared to have little salience for the
population in the central city; the voters apparently agreed with Mayor
Tucker in his belief that there was nothing in the plan for the central
city. Both the protagonists and the antagonists were talking mainly to
the suburbanites, whether they intended to or not. Even so, only the
Post-Dispatch was getting through to as many as 49 per cent. The rest
were not listening.

The respondents who thought they knew an organization's position
were asked why the organization supported (or opposed) the plan.
The most interesting finding is, simply, that a large majority in each
case could not suggest any reason. Of those who did, most reasons
fell in one of two categories—"self-interest" or "the public welfare."
The data are extremely sparse and scattered, but consistency makes

Table 5-5. Recognition of the Positions Taken by Ten Major Organizations Involved in the District Plan Campaign

Organization	Accurate	Inaccurate	Unknown	Not Recognized	Total
St. Louis *Post-Dispatch* (Pro)					
City	28%	9%	69%	5%	101% (85)
County	49	6	43	2	100 (165)
League of Women Voters (Pro)					
City	16	5	26	53	100 (85)
County	20	5	49	26	100 (165)
Metropolitan St. Louis C of C (Pro)					
City	14	6	28	52	100 (85)
County	21	3	49	27	100 (165)
Civic Progress Inc. (Pro)					
City	5	3	6	86	100 (85)
County	3	1	12	85	101 (165)
N.A.A.C.P. (Neutral)					
City	—	5	33	62	100 (85)
County	—	5	54	41	100 (85)

County League of Municipalities (Con)					
City	1	—	16	83	100 (85)
County	11	3	22	64	100 (165)
AFL-CIO Central Labor Council (Con)					
City	3	11	49	37	100 (85)
County	10	19	49	23	101 (165)
Ad Hoc Campaign Organizations					
C.C.C.P. (Pro)					
City	4	2	10	84	100 (85)
County	12	1	13	73	99 (165)
Citizens against the District Plan (Con)					
City	10	2	3	85	100 (85)
County	25	1	11	63	100 (165)
Citizens Committee for Self Government (Con)					
City	3	—	9	89	101 (85)
County	1	1	12	87	101 (165)

them at least intriguing. In general, organizations supporting the plan were judged to do so because of commitment to the public welfare; all opposing were believed to do so mainly because of self-interest.

There is little indication that any of these organizations had a major impact *except* through the mass media. When those who knew the position of an organization were asked where they had learned it, 194 identifications of source were given for the county sample, 63 for the city. (It must be remembered these are not respondents, for each respondent had a chance to identify from zero to ten organizations by position and source of knowledge.) The results are presented in Table 5-6.

Table 5-6. Source of Respondent's Knowledge of Organizational Positions on the District Plan

Source of Knowledge	City Sample	County Sample
Newspapers	43%	68%
Other Mass Media	25	12
Organizational Contact	32	20
	100%	100%
Total Sources	63	194

The campaign was preeminently a mass media campaign. What is more, practically all indications that an organization's position was made known through other means referred to three organizations: the AFL-CIO Central Labor Council, the League of Women Voters, and the Citizen's Committee for City-County Partnership. The first, it will be recalled, did not clearly get its position across anyway. The other two seem to have been the only organizations in the metropolitan area which approached the campaign as anything other than a battle of the media.

The Channels of Communication

The messages, then, from organizations and individuals, traveled almost entirely through four channels; the daily press, the local community papers, television, and radio. Table 5–7 indicates the kind of position attributed by the respondents to each of these media. It is interesting to note that the range of persons who heard *anything* about the plan is so wide, by medium: from 74 per cent in the county who heard via the *Post*, to 25 per cent in the city who heard via their community press. It is clear that, in the suburbs, *all* media were better attended than in the city, but only the *Post* and television reached a majority of the respondents.

Equally impressive is the fact that three-tenths of the suburban residents (who were much more interested, on the average, than city dwellers) did not know the position of the *Post* and the community press. (Yet the community papers took the unprecedented step of publishing Sunday editions against the plan, while the *Post* and the *Globe* carried red banner headlines urging readers to vote for the Plan.)[3] Evidently a large proportion of the readers do not attend carefully enough to know the position taken—even by highly committed media. Such uncertainty is more understandable when we deal with television and radio. The format of these, plus the conventions against editorializing, result in mixed messages—and the mixture is apparent in the large proportion of the respondents who saw the positions of television and radio as "neutral" or "both pro and con." Insofar as there was an effective debate through the media, it came over the air waves.

Of those who did know the positions of the newspapers, however, a majority was correct in each case. Relatively few persons said that the *Post* and *Globe* were against the District Plan; relatively few said the community press was for it. Sixty-two per cent of those in the suburbs who had heard of the plan in the community press said it was against the plan.

Of the suburbanites who had heard through television, 66 per cent said the medium was neutral or mixed. Although the sponsors of the District Plan were apprehensive that the educational television programs had hurt their campaign, it is clear that few persons saw the *medium* as opposed. On the other hand, many persons heard the opposition's arguments *via* the "unbiased" media. As for those who feared

[3] Schmandt, et al., *ibid.*, Chapter IV.

Table 5-7. Positions of the Mass Media on the Issue, as Reported by Respondents

Medium	Percentage Who Heard of Plan Through the Medium	Of Those Who Heard of Plan Through Medium, Percentage Who said the Medium's Position Was:					
		Pro	Neutral	Con	Pro and Con	Unknown
Post-Dispatch						
City	57	50	9	9	1	30
County	74	62	5	3	5	24
Globe-Democrat						
City	30	40	10	13	3	33
County	47	55	6	6	4	28
Community Press						
City	25	12	4	56	—	28
County	50	8	4	68	4	18
Television						
City	57	18	12	—	54	16
County	70	16	27	1	39	17
Radio						
City	26	4	15	4	58	19
County	39	13	25	—	44	18

that the effective policy of the newspapers was blunted by the opposition of some working newsmen to the Plan, it is important to note that five times as many suburbanites said the *Post's* position was pro as said it was neutral, con, or pro and con. Many persons did not read of the plan or hear of it via television or radio; of those who did, many did not know the position of the medium on the issue; but of those who did know, a large majority was correct in every case.

In order to assess crudely the relative weight of the media, we asked some questions forcing the respondents to compare them. Which had the most information on the District Plan? Which was the most trustworthy in its reporting? Which the least? The results are reported in Table 5–8.

Table 5-8. Evaluation of Information and Trustworthiness in the Media by Percentage

Medium	Most Informative?	Which Medium Was: Most Trustworthy?	Least Trustworthy?
Post-Dispatch			
City	21	22	1
County	22	19	10
Globe-Democrat			
City	7	4	4
County	6	7	2
Community			
City	7	9	3
County	11	7	12
Television			
City	7	10	3
County	14	10	6
Radio			
City	3	—	—
County	3	3	3
Don't Know			
City	54	55	89
County	44	54	67

It is clear that many respondents simply could not make up their minds with respect to the questions. It is also clear that the newspapers are the primary sources of information: the dailies account for half the nominations in city and suburbs, with the community press accounting for another fifth. The respondents had difficulty answering the questions concerning "trustworthiness" of media: however, a substantial proportion of those with opinions in the county distrust either the *Post* or the community press. In the case of the *Post*, there is compensation: more than 40 per cent of those with opinions considered it the most trustworthy source of information during the campaign.

The vivid dichotomy between the *Post-Dispatch*, a metropolitan daily with a national reputation, and the little community papers led us to probe their readers' view of them. In a sense, they represent the poles of identification and commitment. One is large-scale and committed to increasing scale of social order in the "metropolitan community." The others are small-scale, devoted to the image of the particular place as community, and jealous of local autonomy. (This opposition is, as we have noted earlier, related to the economic bases

*Table 5-9. Reasons Given for the Positions Taken by the Post and the Community Press by Those Who Knew These Positions (by Percentages)**

They Took the Position Because of:

Medium	Impartiality	"Progress"	The County's (City's) Interest	Self-Interest	Don't Know
Post-Dispatch					
City	13	28	—	15	44
County	10	36	12	10	32
Community Press					
City	—	33	—	—	67
County	2	21	32	14	30

* The proportion knowing the positions were: for the *Post*, 39 per cent in the city, 59 per cent in the county: for the community press, 18 per cent in the city, 42 per cent in the county. The county data are much more trustworthy.

of the two kinds of enterprise, as well as to their wars of words.) Thus it was interesting to discover the motives attributed to each for the positions taken in the campaign: the *Post* was "all-out" for metropolitan government, the community papers were overwhelmingly opposed. Neither medium is accused of "self-interest" in its position by a large proportion of its readers. Sub-regional interest is imputed: the 32 per cent of the county's knowledgeable readers who said the community press took its position because of the "county's interest" were complemented by the 12 per cent which said the *Post's* position was due to the "city's interest." The fact that neither type of divisive interest is mentioned by the city residents may indicate a reason for the tepid nature of the campaign in the ctiy.

The following are some specimen responses, indicating the way the *Post's* position was thought to have come about.

Question: If respondent knows the *Post-Dispatch* position ask: Why do you think they took that position?

Pro:[4] They may have thought that it would benefit the area and was the best plan that had a chance of being passed at this time. I think the *Post* whips up a lot of excitement over local issues to create interest or stimulate interest and sell their paper.

Pro: They thought it was as good a plan as we could have right now. They want the City and County to merger.

Pro: I think the *Post-Dispatch* takes any position they think will do them good in the long run. They'd do anything expedient. It's a half "commie" pink sheet.

Pro: I don't know why. I know they do favor the Democratic party, but I don't know which party the District Plan was beneficial to.

The large number of responses in the suburbs which indicated that the community press position was due to the county's interest broke down to those who spoke of "preservation of local identity" (14 per cent), "maintaining low taxes" (4 per cent), and in more general terms, just protecting the county's interest.

[4] Indicates whether respondent thought *Post* favored, opposed, or was neutral to the plan.

Here are some reasons imputed to the community papers for their *opposition* to the plan.

Question: If respondent knows the community paper position ask: Why do you think they took that position?

Con (Richmond Heights): That was the position of most of the people in the communities where they do business. The livelihood of the newspaper people was involved.

Con (Jennings): They were more interested in the County and after a poll among the residents they decided that it wasn't the right Plan for the community and the people out here were not for it.

Con (St. Louis 15B): Because the community papers are for the people in their communities whole-heartedly. They live among them and work with them and their position was for the benefit of the people.

Con (Webster Grove): It was to the best interest of the local communities to retain their own powers of government.

Con (St. Louis 11A): Because of the possible tax increase issue involved.

A majority of those with opinions, in city and suburbs, saw the *Post* as the protagonist of "progress." Curiously enough, however, many spoke of the community press as taking a stand based upon "progress." Goodness knows what they meant. At all events, few people anywhere gave the community press credit for impartiality. They were seen as completely committed to the fight against the plan.

We should consider, briefly, the efforts of the campaigning organizations to get through by other means than the mass media. These were of four different sorts: phone calls, personal calls (doorbell ringing), mailed leaflets, and speeches or debates at organizational meetings. Results of the telephone campaign, which occupied ladies from the League of Women Voters for many weeks, were recalled by 5 per cent of the suburban respondents, 1 per cent of those in the city. Personal visits were even more rare, 2 per cent and 1 per cent respectively. Leaflets, however, were widely distributed. Thirty-five per cent in each area had seen leaflets on the issues of the campaign. In the city, 21 per cent had seen leaflets pro, 7 per cent con, and the others couldn't remember which side the leaflet was from. In the suburbs the proportions were: 16 per cent pro, 13 per cent con, and 7 per cent who couldn't remember. Eight per cent of the county respondents said the leaflet had been of some help in making up their mind on the issue.

It will be remembered that a major effort went into the series of speeches and debates on public forums. There were, in our sample, 19 reports of attendance at meetings where this had occurred—13 reports from the county, 6 from the city. In four instances the case for the opposition only was made; in six, the proponents only were heard; in eight, both sides were heard. The paucity of these reports leads to a reinforcement of the conclusion that this was a mass media campaign. The endless debates may have affected a few persons in the audience— they could not have made much difference in the outcome of the campaign. We must look further if we are to assign them significance: they may have made a dent when projected on the screen or front page. They may also have fed messages into the informal network of relationships, friendship, kinship, and neighborhoods. We shall discuss these possibilities later.

What Did They Hear?

As a way of getting at the salient messages that came through, we focused on arguments. Such arguments rest on norms and relate to the morality plays of the political culture. Respondents were asked: "What was the best (worst) argument you heard for the District Plan?" and "What was the best (worst) argument you heard against it?" Aside from the intensely committed (who said they heard nothing good, or nothing bad, about the plan) and the indifferent (who heard nothing *either* good or bad), these data provide a set of clues to the normative orders which were invoked by the protagonists and the antagonists of the plan. We shall first detail, briefly, the substance of the arguments cited; then we shall attempt a rough analysis of the normative axes of the discourse; finally, we shall compare the four types of arguments with respect to their sources in the communications flow.

The Best Argument for the Plan. The arguments for the plan were analyzed in two different ways. First, they were categorized with respect to the general problems of government organization and the values attached to change in that organization: these might be called general and formal virtues. Second, wherever specific governmental goods and services were mentioned, these were separately coded. Two tables are necessary to present the results. The general and formal virtues of the plan, as presented to the respondents, appear in Table 5–9.

The reasons given range from the economic fertility of the entire metropolis, through the problem of improving order within the metropolis, to the problems of specific types of governmental goods and services as they affect the neighborhoods, and finally to the cost of government. It is notable that the second and third arguments are, combined, 65 per cent of the arguments given in the city, and 72 per cent of those given by county residents, *in favor of the plan.* Neither the overall good of the metropolis, its prosperity as compared with other American metropolitan areas, nor the pocketbook of the voter is the dominant good implied in these arguments. Order and equity within the metropolis and increased governmental goods and services are more important. It is also important to note that, though the county residents were much better informed and more involved in the campaign, more than twice as many said they heard *nothing good* about the plan. This probably indicates the extent of hard-core opposition to the District Plan among the suburbanites.

Here are specimens of "best arguments heard for the District Plan."

Question: In all the things you heard or read about the District Plan, what was the best argument you heard for it?

It would make the city and county governments better organized and efficient, smoother running.

The taxes was the best I heard for it. (What did you hear about the taxes?) Well, I don't exactly remember, but at the time I remember thinking it would be a good thing.

Most discussion I heard was that if they did have a District Plan they'd combine the police departments instead of going four or five blocks and then running into a different police department.

*Table 5-10. General and Formal Virtues of the District Plan,
As Presented to Respondents in Argument*

Argument	Percentage Mentioning in:	
	City	County
1. The plan increases possi- bilities for progress, in- creased economic opportunities, advantages to entire metropolis.	9	7
2. The plan improves the chances for cooperation among govern- ments, uniform governmental services, righting inequities.	14	15
3. The plan allows for the im- provement of services and solution of specific service problems.	11	21
4. The plan will increase the efficiency of government and lower costs.	2	6
5. All others	3	2
6. Heard nothing good	15	32
7. Heard nothing	47	18
Total	101	101
Number	(81)	(165)

Well I want to tell you something I found very funny. You know at first Mayor Tucker came out for it and then reversed himself. Well, Bill James said on TV that if the politicians were opposed to it, it must be good. It really struck me funny.

To be honest with you I didn't hear anything for it—mostly against it. All the people who ride with me live in the county and we're sort of prejudiced because we're in the city every day and see so many things we don't like. And, we resent the city earnings tax we have to pay.

That there would be City-County coordination. Instead of the city and county fighting it would bring them together under one head. It would help the city people.

There was no best argument. There was nothing good about it. And I heard plenty about it.

That it would solve the problems. This group which would make land-use plans and attempt to bring industry in—and the traffic features. These were the most frequent discussions.

Turning now to the specific governmental goods and services mentioned, we may ask: of all the propaganda that the protagonists made for the plan as a concrete good, what was effective? Which kinds of "problems" as defined by the public reports of the Metropolitan St. Louis Survey (based upon the sample survey of 1957) were seen as problems by the citizens in the context of a campaign to do something about them? Though all the "problems" disclosed as having some currency in 1957 were not targets for the District Plan, several of them were. Traffic and transit coordination and improvement, police coordination together with civil defense organization, industrial development—these were some of the recommendations of the public reports. The first, the state of traffic and transit, was a major source of dissatisfaction in 1957—as it had been instrumental in the beginning of the entire movement.

Specific services were mentioned by a sizable minority of the respondents, especially in the suburbs, but the majority spoke of none. And, of those who did mention specific services, most mentioned traffic and transit in the county or police administration and civil defense in the city. The virtues of the plan as a device for increasing economic fertility (and thereby increasing tax resources for governmental services) were not persuasive to more than a handful of the citizens—although the campaigners devoted considerable energy to this argument. Among the county respondents, dissatisfaction with traffic and transit remained important to half those mentioning services. In some respects it seems to be the motive force behind the entire movement for metropolitan government.

Table 5-11. Improvements in Specific Services Expected from District Plan, as Presented to Respondents in Argument

Specific Service	Percentage Mentioning in:	
	City	County
1. Traffic and Transit	5	16
2. Police and Civil Defense	11	9
3. Planning, Industrial Development	4	4
4. Governmental Administration Improvement	3	2
5. Other	1	1
Sub-Total	24	32
No Specific Service Mentioned	76	68
	100	100
	(81)	(165)

Yet, if we turn back to Table 5–9, it is apparent that many persons thought good arguments had been made for the plan *aside from* the improvement of specific governmental services. Perhaps the "bread and butter" arguments are not the only kind that can get through the sound barriers to the citizens: there is some indication that a general patriotism for the metropolis is of (at least some) importance.

The Worst Argument for the Plan. It was assumed that some arguments made by each side might very well "boomerang"; in the process of trying to please everybody—which seems necessary in a referendum election—one might very well antagonize those who were critical. Thus, with respect to arguments pro and con, the respondent was asked: "And what was the worst argument you heard for (against) it? That is, the one that seemed most phony and made up?" Thirty-two per cent in the county and 13 per cent in the city designated such arguments, made by the protagonists of the District Plan.

By far the most frequently cited "phony" argument was one which ran like this: "That it wouldn't cost more," "That it wouldn't affect taxes," or "That it would be cheaper in the long run." This argument, made by the protagonists, was tied to the assumption that the plan, through improving the economic welfare and tax yield of the metropolis, would not increase the *rate* of taxation in the long run. Twenty-three per cent in the county and 10 per cent in the city suspected its validity. Aside from this one point, only 9 per cent and 3 per cent, respectively, indicated any argument for the plan that seemed phony to them.

Some specimen responses ran as follows:

Question: And in all the things you heard or read about the District Plan, what was the worst argument you heard for it? That is, the argument that seemed phony and made up?

All the arguments seemed phony to me because it was not a good plan. It didn't cover enough territory and would let the politicians add to jobs and/or hang on to them.

Mr. Cervantes made a very phony speech on TV. I said at the time that it was the most ridiculous explanation I had ever heard. For the life of me I can't tell you what he said and what he was for, but I do remember how phony it sounded.

That I was going to get fire and police protection I already had.

Another layer of government which I don't think we need. We have enough now as it is.

It seemed most people in the city are colored and can't pay their bills, and I thought it was just a way to get us to pay their bills. Like the big river front they are building. It is just going to cost so much money and I guess they just wanted us to help pay for that too.

That there would be no increase in any tax we had to pay. The people were really fooled when the Metropolitan Sewer District came into effect. They said it wouldn't increase taxes. It didn't, they gave it a new one.

What I heard over the radio was just sales talk telling what it consisted of. Actually I don't think they readied the people enough for the plan. I actually don't think they expected the District Plan to go through. I think it was a feeler. I don't think they would have known what to do with it if it had gone through. In order to sell anything you have to advertise and I don't think they did enough of that.

The Best Argument against the Plan. The opponents of the District Plan used a large arsenal of arguments. They argued that: the plan was too strong, and too weak; took too much tax money and not enough; would favor city over county and county over city; would weaken local government and would not do away with any local government; would be based on a vague and poorly written (or an exceptionally powerful) charter. The organization of opponents into a city group and a county group, different in origin and without coordination—fighting, indeed, for opposite reasons—further confused the discourse. The very logic of integration reinforced this condition: both city and county would

Table 5-12. Major Faults of the District Plan, as Presented to Respondents In Argument

	Percentage Mentioning In:	
Argument	City	County
1. That cost of government would increase, taxes go up	20	36
2. District too weak to improve services	7	4
3. District too strong	—	2
4. Creates extra layer of government	—	5
5. Local areas will lose power	—	3
6. Would favor city	1	5
7. Would favor county	3	—
8. Technical deficiencies of the charter	5	7
9. Other	3	3
10. Cites authority who is opposed	3	2
11. More good against	1	4
12. All arguments were good	10	11
13. Heard none	47	18
Total	100	100
	(81)	(165)

lose certain powers and resources in the metropolitan district. The *quid pro quo*, of course, was not mentioned by either set of opponents. Instead, they spoke of the city's losses, the county's losses—and nobody spoke of the city's gains when the county lost, or *vice versa*.

The arguments which were heard, and considered strong, by the residents of the two sub-areas are presented in Table 5–11. The most striking aspect of the table is the small number of county residents who heard *no* arguments against the plan. Eighty-two per cent remembered attacks on the plan (compared to 50 per cent who had heard arguments *for* the plan). In the city, however, almost half the respondents had heard no arguments against the plan, while 62 per cent had heard none for it. Thus arguments *against* the District Plan seem to have been much more current, more clearly perceived, and better remembered than arguments for it. (Yet we must remember that the chief source of information was the daily papers—which supported the plan.)

The second major finding is the widespread mention of "higher taxes" as the strongest argument against the plan. Of those who would name a specific argument as the best against the plan, 50 per cent in the county and 47 per cent in the city mentioned this one. As may be seen from the table, other specific arguments had few nominators: the weakness of the district was second mention in the city, and technical deficiencies held this place in the county. In the aggregate, however, 19 per cent in the city and 28 per cent in the suburbs did name other arguments. These reflected the arguments made by opponents, as listed. One might group them in the following fashion: weakness of the district (number 2 in the list); too much government (3, 4, and 5); separatist interests of sub-areas (5 and 6); technical deficiencies (8); and authorities oppose (10). In this scheme, the distribution of Table 5–13 appears. The strength of the district government and the assumption that it was inimical to the particular interests of the county municipalities together counted for most of the nonfiscal arguments recalled in the suburbs. Weakness of the plan and the interests of the city were the corresponding arguments in the city.

Table 5-13. More General Groupings of Arguments Opposing the District Plan

	Percentage Mentioning In:	
Argument	City	County
1. Cost of government would go up	20	36
2. District too weak	7	4
3. District too strong	—	10
4. Separatist interests	4	5
5. Technical deficiencies	5	7
6. Authorities opposed	3	2
7. Other, all good, none heard	61	36
Total	100	100
	(81)	(165)

The Weakest Argument against the Plan. Only 27 per cent of the suburban sample could mention an argument against the plan that they considered dishonest. Half of these said the argument against it on the basis of increase in the cost of government was the "phoniest"— others mentioned were the arguments of the plan's weakness, that it would weaken the local community, and the like. In the city, 15 per cent mentioned poor arguments in opposition: they were distributed in the same fashion.

Thus a minority, around 30 per cent in the suburbs and half as many in the city, could remember arguments against the plan that seemed phony to them. Approximately the same per cent named phony arguments *for* the plan. Whether those on each side simply did not hear the competing arguments, or whether they thought arguments both ways were valid, we cannot now say. It is clear that critics were rare.

Axes of Controversy

These scattered arguments, pro and con, weak and strong, may be grouped under a very few rubrics. In brief, they center around three controversies. First: the issue of increased rationality and "progress" versus increased political control. While a substantial proportion saw increased cooperation as a virtue of the District Plan, minorities saw it as too strong, or too weak: some saw cogency in the argument that it would override local authorities, increase governmental personnel, and become a dictatorship: others saw the same plan as far too weak to really force coordination among local governments.

The second axis unites the issues of service improvement and increased cost of government. The sizable majority which saw the plan as a source of major improvements in traffic, transit, and the like was balanced by a larger number who saw it as entailing tax increases—and they considered this a strong argument against it. On the other hand, quite a few persons considered the argument based on tax increase as a "phony" argument, but only a few persons questioned the likelihood that the plan would indeed improve services.

Finally, there is the axis based on the metropolitan community's future as a whole. A small proportion considered the increased economic opportunity for the city-county *area* as a major virtue in the plan. An even smaller proportion emphasized, however, the differential costs and benefits, to city and to county, of the plan.

These were the major axes of discourse as remembered by the residents. One may speculate about the organization of these propositions in conversation and decision, but our data hardly allow us to go this far. It is clear, however, that the value of political cooperation versus the cost of political subordination among governmental units, and the value of increased services versus the cost in tax increases, summarize logically most of the arguments heard and remembered. Whether or not the controversy took a logical form is, of course, another matter.

How Did They Hear the Arguments?

For each argument reported, the respondent was asked to indicate where he had first heard that argument. The answers amount to a crude index of the effectiveness that each, among several channels of communication, had with respect to carrying arguments still memorable to the respondent. The results are presented in Table 5–14.

Table 5-14. Where Arguments Pro and Con the Plan Were First Heard

For Arguments That Respondent Thought Were:

Medium	Best Pro		Best Con		Worst Pro		Worst Con	
	City	County	City	County	City	County	City	County
Daily papers	3	11	—	2	3	6	—	2
Local papers	—	1	3	3	—	2	1	1
Papers (unspecified)	10	6	1	6	3	4	3	2
(Sub-total)	(13)	(18)	(4)	(11)	(6)	(12)	(4)	(5)
Television	7	8	6	10	1	8	—	2
Radio	—	2	—	2	—	2	—	2
(Sub-total)	(7)	(10)	(6)	(12)	(1)	(10)	(0)	(4)
Formal Meetings	1	4	3	2	—	1	—	1
Informal talk	6	9	11	21	1	7	5	10
(Sub-total)	(7)	(13)	(14)	(23)	(1)	(8)	(5)	(11)
Don't Know	11	13	12	21	4	10	5	7
No Arguments	62	47	64	32	89	61	86	72
Total	100%	101%	100%	99%	101%	101%	100%	99%
	(81)	(165)	(81)	(165)	(81)	(165)	(81)	(165)

It is clear that the best arguments *for* the plan were preponderantly transmitted by the mass media: 74 per cent in the city and 70 per cent in the county who could remember the origins of such arguments mentioned the media. The best arguments *against* the plan, however, were more apt to have been heard through informal talk and conversation: of those who remembered arguments, 60 per cent in the city and 46 per cent in the county mentioned such sources. Thus it appears that the campaign for the plan relied preponderantly upon the media; that against it was not quite so effective in this respect. This was more than balanced, however, by the large proportion which had heard good arguments against the plan in private conversation—23 per cent and 14 per cent in county and city respectively. This must be compared with the 13 per cent and 7 per cent, in these areas, who had heard good arguments *for* the plan in this way. The mass media were "working" for the plan, the conversational ferment against it. It is also important to note the variations in the effectiveness of the various media. Consistent with earlier findings (see "The Channels of Communication"), television was cited as the origins of both arguments pro and arguments con. The papers, however (and the dailies predominated), were origins of the best argument for the plan in 13 per cent of the cases in the city, 18 in the county, and origins of best arguments against in only 4 per cent of the city cases and 11 per cent of those in the county.

With respect to the worst arguments pro and con ("the most phony and dishonest"), there is an important variation. The worst arguments *for* the plan, in the judgment of the respondent, were overwhelmingly imputed to the media. In the county, where 30 per cent reported such "phony" arguments, they assigned their contact with them to the media in 70 per cent of the cases. With respect to "phony" arguments against the plan, however, the media and face-to-face interaction were equally responsible. The chief reason for this difference is the much larger proportion reporting phony arguments *for* the plan (compared to those against it) as originating in the mass media.

The importance of the communication of arguments through informal talk leads us to consider the persons who originated messages.

After learning where the respondent had heard a given argument, the interviewer asked "And who made that argument?" The personal nature of the relationships through which arguments were often transmitted is apparent in Table 5–15.

In the suburbs, where our sample is most trustworthy and the campaign was most lively, 31 per cent remembered the source of the argument against the plan which they considered strongest. Of these, more than half (18 per cent) referred to a specific relative, friend, or neighbor. The network of informal relationships and the conversational ferment carried a large proportion of the messages critical of the plan. However, it should be noted that the identified sources of all arguments (pro and con, good and bad) are usually specific persons—relatives, friends, and neighbors, in city *and* suburb. The only exception of any significance is the strongest argument against the plan as recalled by suburban respondents: 8 per cent heard it from public officials (and this source was, really, Mayor Tucker); 6 per cent attributed the argument to him.

A Provisional Tally

The campaign for the District Plan mobilized a few organizations and a fairly large number of the reputationally involved. It "worked" chiefly through two channels: the projection of arguments through reports of activity in the media, and direct messages addressed to the population—also via the media. The central city dailies were the major source of single-minded supporting arguments. Many persons, however, particularly in the suburbs, distrusted the aims and interests of the *Post-Dispatch* and the *Globe-Democrat* on the issue. The campaign was effective in communicating a number of arguments to a substantial minority in the city and to half the county respondents.

The campaign against the District Plan, insofar as it was effective, worked through these *and other* channels. The major channels were the reflections of arguments by the "Big Mules" in opposition as reported in the daily press, direct argument to the voters by television and in the television debates, and the single-minded commitment of the

Table 5-15. Sources of Arguments Pro and Con

Source of Argument	Arguments Pro				Arguments Con			
	Best		Worst		Best		Worst	
	City	County	City	County	City	County	City	County
Relatives, neighbors, friends	5	7	1	6	7	18	4	8
Officials of government	1	1	—	2	—	8	—	2
Other: organizations, news writers	1	4	1	4	1	4	—	2
(Sub-total)	(7)	(12)	(2)	(12)	(8)	(31)	(4)	(12)
Other (scattered)	1	3	—	2	5	4	—	1
Don't Know	20	27	6	19	14	22	5	10
No Information	72	58	91	67	73	43	90	76
Total	100	100	99	100	100	100	99	99
	(81)	(165)	(81)	(165)	(81)	(165)	(81)	(165)

local community press. While these sources of argument were important, there is some indication that they were not the media that carried the day. A great proportion had heard the strongest negative arguments from friends, neighbors, and relatives (particularly in the suburbs). This leads one to suspect that opposing normative systems, already existing in the neighborhoods and local communities, were simply activated by the official structuring of "metropolitan integration" as an issue. Another reason for believing this to be so is the weakness of the link between those who publicly fought against the plan and the citizens who decided against it.

Because of the impressive proportion who heard the strongest arguments against the plan from informal conversation with relatives, friends, and neighbors, it seems useful to look in some detail at what they report about these conversations.

6

Political Conversation:
Who Talked to Whom about
What—and What Came of It?

In approaching the general conversational ferment over the issue, several questions emerge. What kinds of social relationships were the carriers for the communication flow? What was the tone, negative or positive? What did the respondent believe he carried away from such conversation? Did he feel he had been able to change anyone's mind? Experience has indicated that most informal relationships may be categorized as one of the following: (1) kinfolk, (2) neighbors, (3) fellow workers on the job, and (4) other friends. Therefore the interviewer carried on a brief, structured conversation with the respondent about each set of associations.

First the respondent was asked, with respect to a relationship, "Was there any talk about the District Plan among your ———?" And if there was, he was asked "How many times do you suppose the subject came up? Was it discussed very often, occasionally, or very seldom?" The results are presented in Table 6–1.

The greater saliency of the topic among the suburbanites is striking. Equally striking are the *loci* of the conversations. On *a priori* grounds one would have predicted that most conversation would occur with neighbors. People would appear to have more common interests in the district plan with them than with anyone else, and neighbors, being near at hand, would seem most accessible.[1] It is clear, instead, that the plan was least likely to come up as a topic in neighborly conversation. The quantitatively most important settings for conversations were on the job with work associates and at home among the kinfolk. In the suburbs, 30 per cent had talked about the plan at least occasionally with their fellow workers: 36 per cent had discussed the plan this frequently with relatives.

Table 6-1. Frequency of Discussion among Kinfolk, Neighbors, Fellow Workers, and Friends (in Percentage)

	District Plan Was Discussed:			
Relationship	Often	Occasionally	Seldom	Never
1. Kinfolk				
City	6	10	5	79
County	13	23	12	53
2. Neighbors				
City	5	7	1	87
County	4	15	10	71
3. Work associates				
City	5	16	12	77
County	17	13	11	59
4. Other friends				
City	4	7	1	88
County	5	18	8	69

What are we to make of this finding? A first proposition would be based on sheer quantity of interaction. People who work spend a great deal of time in interaction with fellow workers; people with

[1] Though not all suburban residents are involved in their neighborhood, a majority (60 per cent) visit with neighbors regularly at least once a month, and a large minority do so several times a week. See Scott Greer, "The Social Structure and Political Process of Suburbia: An Empirical Test," *Rural Sociology*, Vol. 27, No. 4, pp. 438–459.

relatives spend much of their free time among them. Thus there is more opportunity to talk: one talks about many things, but frequently about whatever is currently "news." As we have seen, the District Plan was an important topic in the mass media for several months.

A second hypothesis is addressed to the related question: why did so few suburban residents, neighborly as they are, discuss the issue even occasionally in their neighborhood? The hypothesis rests upon a simple proposition about neighboring and the neighborhood as a structure: the minimal ordering of behavior in the neighborhood is very useful to each household, but in respect to matters which are quite divorced from larger political concerns. This is because the introduction of *divisive issues* into neighborly relations is a threat to the small-scale social order of the neighborhood—the family's *modus vivendi* with its "nigh dwellers." The District Plan was such a divisive issue.

Work associates, however, are not likely to come from the same neighborhood. Indeed, they come from various municipalities within the metropolis. The issues become more public and divorced from a common, intense commitment to the neighborhood. Talk can become "objective" and "casual." Thus, in the conversational mill of office or factory, the District Plan was not so divisive of basic relations. The family is at the other extreme; it is a unit less impervious to division by most larger, public issues.

We were intrigued by the frequency with which the issue had been discussed on the job, and for this reason asked the respondent "How did the District Plan happen to come up?" In both city and county the usual response was simply "in general conversation." (This accounted for about two-thirds of the responses.) In the county, the bulk of the other responses could be summarized: it came up "in discussions of current events as reported by the mass media." This, of course, supports the interpretation we have just made.

With respect to conversation on the plan among "other friends," the respondent was asked *where* such conversations took place. The results are given in Table 6–2. The greater interest in the subject among suburbanites is accompanied by a greater spread of associational sites. Sixteen per cent reported conversations on the plan in such

Table 6-2. The Locus of Conversations on the District Plan with "Other Friends"

Locus	Percentage of Such Conversations in:	
	City	County
Visits in home	5	8
Parties		8
Organizational meetings	1	6
Casual interaction in public places	4	8
Everywhere	1	1
(Sub-total)	(11)	(31)
No Information	89	69
Total	100	100
	(81)	(165)

informal settings as visits and parties. Eight per cent discussed it in casual interaction at markets, parking lots, bus stops, and the like. The plan was clearly a topic of some saliency in the conversational stream of the suburbs.

Turning next to the general tone of the conversation, the interviewer asked: Was the talk usually favorable, unfavorable, or mixed? It is clear that most conversations were largely inimical to the campaign for the District Plan. Considering first those who designated the conversations as either unfavorable or favorable, the unfavorable talk predominates. In no case did more than one-sixth of those reporting conversations say that the talk was generally favorable to the plan. On the other hand, 60 per cent of those in the suburbs who had discussed the plan with their neighbors said the talk was usually unfavorable.

Only with neighbors was a majority of the conversations unfavorable, but this does not mean a large proportion of any set of conversations was favorable. The others were simply "mixed." This is what one would expect, if political conversation were indeed a working out of interests and policy through discussion and persuasion. Two-thirds

Table 6-3. The General Tone of Conversation on the District Plan (by Percentage)

Relationship	The talk was generally:			
	Favorable	Mixed	Unfavorable	(Inappropriate)
1. Kinfolk				
City	5	10	6	79
County	4	23	20	53
2. Neighbors				
City	1	5	7	87
County	3	8	16	73
3. Work Associates				
City	3	10	16	71
County	2	15	19	64
4. Other friends				
City	1	6	5	88
County	—	21	12	67

of those talking with "other friends" reported that both sides were usually heard; half of those who talked with relatives or work associates said the conversations were usually mixed; only 30 per cent said the talks with their neighbors were usually mixed.

If the tentative explanation for the lower rate of conversation about the plan in the neighborhood is correct, an explanation follows. In brief, if the "peace" of the neighborhood is a paramount norm, and if the majority tends to oppose the plan, there would be strong reasons for those who support the plan to keep their mouths closed. This would seem to have happened, for there is no reason to believe that most neighborhoods were completely barren of supporters or, at least, those with "an open mind." Instead, one suspects that the dominant majority, and its noise, effectively silenced opposition. Thus the talk in the neighborhoods was not often "mixed"—it was usually "unfavorable." In brief, the paramount norms of the neighborhood system probably tend to suppress divisive issues; when they arise, it is likely the norms work toward the suppression of minority opinion.

Such conversation could be expected, at least, to keep the topic "alive." We wanted, however, to get some notion of the effects of political conversation. Table 6–4 summarizes answers to two questions: "Did you learn anything from these conversations?" And, if "yes": "How was that?"

Table 6-4. What They Learned from Political Conversations (by Percentage)

| | Respondent said he learned: | | | |
Relationship	Facts about Plan	Other Points of View	Nothing	There Was No Talk
1. Kinfolk				
City	4	10	7	79
County	11	9	27	53
2. Neighbors				
City	4	4	6	86
County	5	5	17	73
3. Work Associates				
City	5	5	20	70
County	6	7	24	63
4. Other Friends				
City	7	4	1	88
County	4	8	20	68

The respondents were most likely to report that they had learned something from the conversations with kinfolk. Considering chiefly the suburban sample, where there were more conversations (as well as interviews), 44 per cent of those who participated said they had learned from the conversations, while the other three categories of relationship were all within two percentage points of 35 per cent. The two major categories of learning were "information about the plan" and "what other people think."

Here we list some specimen responses to the question on what they learned for each type of social relationship.

Questions 9d, 10d, 11e, 12e. Was there any talk about the District Plan among your kinfolks and family (9d), neighbors (10d), work associates (11e), other friends (12e)? Did you learn much from such conversations—how is that?

A. Family

What the plan stood for. Some saw objections that I didn't see right away and they pointed them out to me. (What objections were those?) That we would have to pay for services twice that we are already paying for such as police and fire protection and schools.

Well, I think there were many things I was not clear on and my family straightened me out.

My daughter came home from her office and many of the things said there were because of a political plum. I think she changed her mind after we discussed it.

Many of them were grossly misinformed. I think somehow the publicity on this matter did not get through to even many of those who were really interested.

B. Neighbors

I learned that most people were for merging rather than keeping it in separate small villages or townships.

I had my mind made up right away—no one could have changed it.

It was really a repetition of what I had already heard or read.

Most people were against it but didn't know why.

I learned a lot of people had a lot of wrong ideas or misconceptions about what the District Plan was.

C. Work Associates

I learned their viewpoints. Mostly we were concerned about taxes.

To begin with (it was) one way I learned exactly what the points were. They announced them on the radio and we discussed them. We also talked about where the seat of government would be—in Clayton or City Hall, and what type of government it would be—city management, or just what.

You always learn from talking to others; I don't remember anything in particular though.

D. Friends

They did not seem to know much. They could not seem to see where we would derive any benefits and thought we should leave well enough alone.

I learned that many of these small communities should go together. They're so small we don't get the services we should out of them.

Very little information offered that I didn't already know.

The most striking aspect of these findings is the small proportion who said they had learned *anything* from the relatively frequent conversations they had heard or sustained. One is inclined to explain this by the very casual nature of such conversations. The avoidance of intense commitment to ideological positions in informal interaction seems to be a common pattern in American society.[2] The findings would support a generalization from national voting studies to the effect that, after early polarization on an issue, very few persons are apt to "learn" the opposing side's arguments. Either they do not hear them, or they discount them. The "open-minded, independent voter" seems to be a relatively rare bird even in nonpartisan elections on local issues.

How They Saw Others Acting

This general preponderance of conversation inimical to the plan was accompanied by a preponderance (among respondents who thought they knew how their friends had voted) of those who believed they'd voted against it. Thirty-six per cent in the city and 64 per cent in the county thought they knew how many of their friends had voted.

Only a minority saw most of their friends as voters in the referendum. They were also asked to estimate the general feeling, among their friends, about the District Plan. In both city and county, those who thought they knew their friends' position saw them as overwhelmingly against it.

[2] See, for example, the studies of friendship and values carried out by the Social Science Research Council summer seminar in 1956, under the direction of Robin Williams. (*Friendship and Social Values*, Eugene, Oregon, 1956, mimeographed)

Table 6-5. How Many of Their Friends They Thought Had Voted

| How Many Voted? | Percentage in: | |
	City	County
Most	21	38
Some	4	6
Few	11	19
Don't Know	43	29
Inappropriate	21	7
	100	99
	(81)	(165)

The proportion opposed, if we take these figures literally, is actually much higher than the vote against the plan. However, there may be a certain adjustment of perception to revealed reality—after an election people tend to give more weight to the winning side.

Table 6-6. How They Thought Their Friends Had Felt about the Plan

| Were they mostly for it, mostly against it, or split about even? | Percentage in: | |
	City	County
Mostly for it	5	4
Split about even	14	18
Mostly against it	22	42
Don't Know	26	16
Inappropriate	33	20
	100	100
	(81)	(165)

Another possibility is that many persons who are committed to a generally unpopular cause will overestimate the amount of opposition to that cause. If it is true that minority opinion tends to be suppressed in conversations, it is plausible for anyone to overestimate the predominance of the majority definition. At any rate, after the event the great majority of our respondents reported an overwhelming sentiment against the plan among their friends. This was probably the visible social fact for them during the campaign: its effects we cannot estimate at this time.

One way of approaching the meaning of the campaign to the voter is to ask him (1) who he thought favored the plan and (2) why he thought they did so. This should give us some notion of his interpretation of the plan's value for different groups, realistically and in terms of symbolic attractiveness. The answers to the first question are presented in Table 6–7. It should be clear that the specific nature of these voters' reasons for favoring the plan is not given in this table. Instead, we have a crude measure of the respondent's *concept* of those who are its supporters.

Here are some responses in the words of the interviewees.

Question. What kinds of voters do you think favored the District Plan? What kinds of people, that is, would vote for it? Why do you think so?

The middle classes. They wouldn't be too concerned about the possible increase in taxes and progress of the city. Five years from now they might be in Alaska.

Property owners in the City of St. Louis who would personally gain by having the plan passed.

People who are interested in improving the whole county. They don't have enough money in small towns to have everything they want done.

Middle- or upper-class people who tend to look to the future of the community.

Most likely tenants. They don't have to pay the taxes.

People who have to ride the public transportation because they could get downtown faster.

Since so many of the colored from the city come out here to work they would vote for it and they would feel united with us in the county.

People who work in the city and have to pay the earnings tax. It might behoove them to incorporate the city and the county.

Table 6-7. Kinds of Voters Seen as Favoring the District Plan (by Percentages)

| Type of Voter | Percentage Said to Favor Plan in: | |
	City	County
1. By political orientation:		
"the civic minded"	11	23
2. By economic strata		
Business people	4	7
Upper income	—	3
Middle income	1	2
Lower income, non-property owner	11	8
(Sub-total)	(16)	(20)
3. By urban sub-region		
County people	8	2
City people	4	4
(Sub-total)	(12)	(6)
4. By career interest		
Political gains	4	3
Economic gains	4	9
(Sub-total)	(8)	(12)
5. By political competence		
Incompetent	3	7
Competent	1	2
(Sub-total)	(4)	(9)
6. Negroes	—	1
7. Other	3	3
8. No Information	47	27
	101	101
	(81)	(165)

Middle class people. There is a majority of them for one thing, and they seem to have a lot to do with all phases of the city life. Some live in the city and work in the county and some live in the county and work in the city. I think it is the working class of people who would vote for it.

First, few respondents emphasize the matter of personal competence. Only 12 per cent in the county mentioned it at all. Nor was immediate self-interest mentioned often. Instead, the attributes most emphasized were those based upon social position, sub-region of residence, or civic-minded orientation to the polity. The scattered references to income-class groups are somewhat puzzling. It is clear, however, that very few people considered *middle-income voters to favor* the plan. Instead, some interests of businessmen and the renting population is implied. Scattered evidence indicates that the first were considered to have collective economic interest (probably related to the fate of the downtown shopping center) and the second were thought to escape the costs of an increased property tax. Some elucidation of the findings is possible through a consideration of the next question: why did the respondent think these classes supported the plan?

Table 6-8. Reasons Assigned to Those Who Supported the District Plan

Reason	Percentage Who Supported for this Reason in:	
	City	County
1. Community interest	16	26
2. Divisive interests		
Monetary	11	8
Political	2	3
Racial	—	1
Other	5	8
(Sub-total)	(18)	(20)
3. Competence		
Competent	—	2
Incompetent	—	2
Irresponsible	9	12
(Sub-total)	(9)	(16)
4. Other	3	1
5. Inappropriate	55	36
	101	99

When the probing question was added, it became apparent that a larger proportion of the respondents accounted for the support of the District Plan as a result of the political competence of the voters. The chief difference was the substantial proportion mentioning "irresponsibility" in one form or the other. In brief, 22 per cent of the county respondents who would hazard "reasons" (16 per cent of the total) gave incompetence or irresponsibility.

It is striking that very few persons mentioned race at all. Nor did many talk in explicitly political terms. Instead, they dealt with economic interests, political responsibility, and civic-minded desires for community progress. (These three accounted for, respectively, 80 per cent of the "reasons" given by the city sample, 72 per cent by the county respondents.) Similar conclusions emerge when the respondents indicate the kinds of voters they thought *opposed* the District Plan. If we allow simple conservatism ("don't change a thing") to stand as an orientation to the metropolitan community, we can say that the same *kinds* of reasons for opposition were imputed to the voters who opposed as were assigned those who supported the plan. These are the "cost-benefit" dilemma, the conservative-progressive division, and the competence-incompetence imputation. It is important to note, however, that this table is not comparable to Table 6–7, in which we asked the respondents why they thought given types took certain positions. It is, once more, only a crude estimate of the way they conceived the opposition to the plan as a social fact.

Specimen responses to the question follow.

Question. And what kinds of voters opposed the plan? This is, what kinds of people would vote against it?

Those who do own their own property. They have more responsibility. They are more likely to stay put because they have their own homes. They are more permanent, more settled.

People like myself. I mean people who feel like I do about this. People who want their communities to stay like they are and not get all swallowed up in a big mass. When you get too big, they'd all be the same.

Table 6-9. Kinds of Voters Seen As Opposing the District Plan

Type of Voter	Percentage Said to Oppose Plan in:	
	City	County
1. Those who like things as they are	5	16
2. By economic strata		
Property owners	30	24
Upper income	1	1
Middle income	—	1
Lower income	3	4
(Sub-total)	(34)	(30)
3. By urban sub-region		
County people	3	4
City people	1	—
4. By career interest		
Political	4	6
5. Those who thought Plan inadequate	4	3
6. By political competence		
Competent	1	8
Incompetent	4	9
(Sub-total)	(5)	(17)
7. Other	4	2
8. Inappropriate	41	22
	101	100
	(81)	(165)

People that like simple community life. That is why they moved to the county in the first place.

Local political seekers or the politically ambitious in local community politics and their friends.

Property owners. They were satisfied with their own schools, traffic plan, and fire and police protection.

Isolationists. Let me tell you they give the argument, "I moved out of the city to get away from the niggers." My own niece said that! And she's got one of the biggest nigger communities right out here next to her. Kinloch Park. You have to go through Kinloch Park to get to Ferguson. It don't make sense. And, second, taxes. They say the taxes in the city are too high when for a fact, the per capita tax in St. Louis is $117, out here it's somewhere between $158 and $185.[3]

Three types: those that don't want their taxes raised, those that were opposed to any change, and those like me who wanted something better.

In summary, only a minority of the city sample thought that at least a few of their friends had voted in the referendum, compared to about two-thirds of the suburbanites. In both city and county, the great majority of those who would estimate said that the opinions among their friends were mostly opposed to the plan, a substantial minority said the opinions were mixed, and very few thought opinions were mostly favorable to the plan. Voters who supported the plan were believed to be responding to the norms of civic interest, to the interests of their stratum, to personal interest, or in terms of their personal competence. Those who opposed the plan were responding to the conservative norms ("better the evil that is known"), economic stratum interests, or in terms of their personal competence. Civic-minded voters were seen as opposing those who feared change and higher taxes.

What Did They Learn about the Plan?

A large majority of the respondents had heard about the District Plan—nearly 80 per cent in the city, and 93 per cent in the county. Substantial majorities had heard through stories in the *Post-Dispatch* and programs on television; substantial minorities, through stories in the *Globe-Democrat* and the local community press, and through programs on the local radio stations. In general, the respondents felt that the media were trustworthy—though the *Post* and television were considered most informative. Half the city respondents and an overwhelm-

---

[3] Sic. The area in question is an incorporated all-Negro municipality, named Kinloch.

ing majority in the suburbs could give "strong" arguments on the issue; they heard these arguments through the mass media but also, significantly, through informal talk and conversation about the plan. In the county particularly, the conversational ferment about the issue reached a large proportion of the people. Sixty-four percent of the county respondents recalled specific arguments *con*, 39 per cent recalled arguments *pro*. (Table 5–12).

These facts lead us to ask a few simple questions about their information. What did the public think was in the District Plan? What were their own specific evaluations of it—the weak points and the strong points? And how do they feel about the general enterprise, whether or not they supported this particular charter for metropolitan reorganization of government? What do they think of future metropolitan government plans?

Information

The campaigners for the District Plan had the task of communicating a complex blueprint for a new system of metropolitan government. Because of their own definitions of saliency, as well as the issues thrust upon them by public response to the plan, certain kinds of information were crucial. The first, and probably most important to the protagonist, was a clear statement of the increased benefits to the metropolitan community. In other words, what kinds of services was the plan supposed to render to the citizens? As we have seen earlier (Chapter 4), the campaigners spent a great many words describing traffic and transit problems, problems of industrial development, and the need for integration of other specific public services.

Because of the massive emphasis upon taxes by their opponents, which they had expected, considerable attention was given to the low level of additional taxes required. The initial cost was to be at most only 50 cents on the 100 dollars of evaluation, for an estimated total of around 18 or 20 million dollars.

Concern for the probable resistance of those favoring local autonomy and government close to the people led to two emphases: (1) upon the government of the metropolitan district by a council and a president, both elected by the metropolitan population, and (2) upon the fact that the new government would not abolish any existing government, but would merge the Metropolitan Sewer District, a nonelective special district government.

Thus the strategy of the protagonists was to place a heavy emphasis on the benefits to be gained, to counter arguments of expense and massive power with information showing the relatively modest powers actually granted the district in the new charter. Let us examine the degree to which they succeeded in communicating—much less in persuading (Table 6–10).

Table 6-10. Services Imputed to the New Metropolitan District Government

Service	First Opportunity	Second Opportunity	Third Opportunity	Total Mentions*
Percentage Naming at:				
1. Traffic, transit				
City	9	3	4	16
County	21	16	12	49
2. Police, civil defense				
City	9	3	1	12
County	24	11	8	43
3. Industrial, economic development				
City	3	1	3	7
County	3	2	1	6
4. Zoning and planning				
City	—	—	—	—
County	3	2	1	6
5. Sewers				
City	4	7	9	12
County	2	5	5	12

The major services to be affected by the plan are included in this table, if one allows the reorganization of tax assessments as falling under heading 6. It is clear that only 38 per cent in the city could name even one service to be affected. In the county, however, 64 per cent could name at least one, while half the county population could name two, and 40 per cent could name three. A larger proportion in the suburbs could name three services than could name *one* in the city sample. The greater saliency of the issues and effectiveness of the campaign in the suburbs is once more apparent.

Less than half the suburban sample agreed in naming *any one* specific service, however. Only two services were named by more than 12 per

Table 6-10 *(Continued)*

Service	Percentage Naming at:			
	First Opportunity	Second Opportunity	Third Opportunity	Total Mentions*
6. General efficiency, progress				
City	9	1	—	10
County	12	2	2	16
7. Other				
City	6	—	—	6
County	2	1	1	4
8. Nothing				
City	9	—	—	9
County	10	—	—	10
9. Inaccurate				
City	—	6	4	10
County	7	15	5	27
10. Don't Know				
City	53	70	79	
County	19	36	36	

* Adds to more than unity because each respondent could name up to three services.

cent of the county population sample—these were traffic and transit, and police and civil defense. Otherwise, the messages simply did not get through to most listeners. In fact, the third most common response in the county was the naming of a service which would *not* be affected by the plan; the fourth most common was "don't know." The "carrot" was not very effectively presented to the donkey; how well the donkey would have liked it is difficult to ascertain.

It is true that many of those interviewed did not vote. Still, thirty per cent of the city sample reported they *had* voted. At a maximum estimate, assuming that the voters were best informed, only a few more than half could have known that the plan provided for improved traffic and transit systems, only 40 per cent that it applied to police and civil defense, and to the sewerage system, 20 per cent that it affected zoning and planning, and industrial development. In the county, 60 per cent of the sample reported they had voted. Using the same logic, a large majority of voters *could* have known that the traffic and transit system and police and civil defense would be affected. But only a small minority could have known that the plan would change (and hopefully improve) the four other major services of government.

It would appear that the suburban voters were deciding on a District Plan which was, to them, primarily a mechanism to improve traffic, transit, and public safety in the metropolitan area. We could not determine what the city voters thought they were voting for or against.

Taxes. As we have seen earlier, the issue of increased taxes was one of the strong weapons used by the opposition, one the protagonists had to address again and again in debate and public hearing. The provisions of the plan were simple. The district could tax up to 50 cents on the 100-dollar evaluation (for a total of around $20,000,000) with further increases possible *only* through referendum vote. (This was considered a weak aspect of the plan by many "experts," since the Metropolitan Sewer District would probably lose its fiscal powers with merger into the District Plan). Modest as it was, however, the taxing power of the district was a distinctly frightening aspect to many voters. Let us see what they thought the district could do to their property taxes.

Here are some verbatim transcriptions of typical responses:

Question. And how much property tax would (will) we have to pay to the district each year?

At least $20 on each auto and some more on our property.

I don't know. They talked about this all the time, but I just can't remember. (How much?) Yeah, a considerable amount. It was based on property value I think, but I can't remember the rate. But it was plenty.

We always pay too much taxes for everything and this would be no different. None. I think ours would be a lot lower in the city.

I'm sure it was an increase, but the amount I am not sure of.

I don't know the amount. They'd tell us none till they got us and then they'd really give it to us.

That was a hot potato, a political football. Those against it (the District Plan) said it could be as much as 15 million, but the tax situation wasn't definite. I do think we'd have an increase in property tax, however.

I don't know, but it was plenty.

Table 6-11. Estimates of New Property Tax to Be Paid to the District

Estimate of Taxes	Respondent's Estimate in Percentage:	
	City	County
1. Correct	3	10
2. Incorrect (larger increase)	11	15
3. Don't know but would be increased	10	10
4. Don't know at all	76	65
	100	100
	(81)	(165)

In general, the answer is clear. They hadn't any notion of the tax provisions in the charter for the new district. The effectiveness of the opposition, then, might be considered to lie only in the confusion they had created. Even if we include the correct, the incorrect, and the vague, only half of the suburban sample which said they had voted could have had *any* kind of notion of the plan's effects upon their taxes. The protagonists of the District Plan did not communicate on this essential point: the opponents had little reason to educate the public. Most of the sample could have considered tax raises only through vague apprehensions.

Government of the District. First the Metropolitan St. Louis survey and then the Board of Freeholders spent many hours of discussion over the basic political question: who shall wield power? They debated the merits of a borough system versus a federal system using existing units of government, an elected official versus appointed official as chief administrator, the boundaries of boroughs, and the like. Their final plan included a legislative branch partly elected from newly drawn borough limits and partly at large in city and in county, and a chief executive elected at large. Thus a key question was: "And who is supposed to govern this metropolitan district?" We have tried to separate degrees of vagueness in Table 6–12.

Table 6-12. Respondents' Notions of the Metropolitan District's Governance

	Percentage responding in:	
Scheme Adumbrated	City	County
1. Board elected by districts (something like plan)	3	6
2. Board, council, aldermen, from different areas	9	7
3. Board, council, aldermen, constituencies unnamed	6	18
4. City, county, or city and county	—	6
5. Completely inaccurate	14	7
6. Don't Know	69	57
	101	101
	(81)	(165)

Here are sample responses in the interviewees' own words:

Question. And who is (was) supposed to govern this metropolitan district?
Same. It wasn't supposed to change in the governing.
Each mayor and his board of aldermen.

The city would annex the county and the city office would govern.

I believe there was only about four members appointed for about four years.

I don't know how long they was to run.

I don't know. I imagine St. Louis would.

It was supposed to be under a split deal then. Five men or three men, an uneven number so they could work.

By the most generous estimate, combining 1 and 2 in the table, only 40 per cent who voted in the city could have known what kind of government they opposed or supported. The comparable proportion in the county (presumably more sensitive to change of power) is about 20 per cent of those voting. Whatever weight was given to presumed public response to the plan by its drafters was, very likely, a "ghost weight," based on assumptions of rational communication which hardly seem tenable.

Abolishing Existing Units. We have noted earlier that the Freeholders' fear of abolishing existing units of government was based on the belief that the citizens would resent this loss of their existing municipalities. The small suburban units were seen as familiar, trusted, "close to the people." The District Plan did not abolish any incorporated municipality in the area, or change the boundaries of school districts, fire districts, or other special districts. Only the unpopular and little-understood Metropolitan Sewer District would be abolished; it would merge with the general metropolitan government.

Table 6-13. Respondents' Notions as to How Many Governments Would Be Abolished

	Percentage Responding in:	
Response Was:	City	County
1. Accurate	14	27
2. Inaccurate (some to all)	10	21
3. Vague	4	3
4. Don't know	72	49
	100	100

With this important aspect of the plan in mind, the respondent was asked: "How many governments would the District Plan abolish?" The results confirm our suspicion that many persons never learned, during the campaign, what it was about.

Their misapprehensions are clear in the following verbatim quotations.

Questions. How many governments would (did) the District Plan abolish? And what government(s) is (are) that (those)?

All the small communities: Jennings, Flordell Hills, all of them.

Well they wouldn't be abolished really. They'd be combined. There would be fewer and larger ones.

All in the county. All the mayors and councilmen of the county districts would eventually have to go.

I imagine quite a few. I don't know. Some of these little . . . well like we have a chief of police and a mayor in all these little communities and it would have taken these out.

Both city and county. There would be nine or eleven instead of two like we have now.

As low as was the proportion, this question seems to have elicited more correct responses than any other save that dealing with services. Oddly enough, however, the incorrect responses are almost as frequent as the correct ones. Thus in the suburbs, for each two persons who did not know anything about the issue, another would know and be correct, another would think he knew and be incorrect or extremely vague.

In summary: Around one-half of the county sample knew of two major services which would be affected by the new district. Ten per cent knew its tax provisions. Thirteen per cent had a fairly accurate knowledge of its governance. Twenty-seven per cent knew that it would not abolish existing municipal government units. The rest was ignorance. In light of these findings it may seem folly to ask how the respondents evaluated the District Plan. However, Americans routinely make value judgments on public policy which they fail to understand in the most minimal sense. These judgments affect the governance of the country.

Evaluation

Despite their erratic knowledge of the plan, a majority of those with opinions in each area found something good to say about it. Of the total, 43 per cent in the city and 61 per cent in the county mentioned something they liked about the District Plan. Though only a minority could name any one specific service, a slight majority in the county named one or the other of the five services affected by the plan. A small proportion mentioned structural improvements, general goods to be brought about by reorganization of the governmental machinery. Forty per cent in the county and 57 per cent in the city did not (or could not) name any aspect of the plan they had liked. In the light of previous data, these results are not surprising.

The respondents were also asked "And what were its weak points? What did you dislike about the District Plan?" It was hypothesized

Table 6-14. What They Liked about the District Plan

Aspect of Plan	Percentage Total Mentioning* (Three Opportunities)	
	City	County
1. Specific Services Named		
Police	20	27
Traffic-transit	6	14
Zoning, planning	5	4
Others (sewers, civil defense)	7	8
(Sub-total)	(38)	(53)
2. Structural Coordination	1	9
Economies	4	—
(Sub-total)	(5)	(9)
3. Other	11	13
4. Inaccurate	2	6
5. Nothing Good	6	12
6. No Information	51	28

* Adds to more than unity because each respondent could name up to three aspects.

that, if the arguments in the air had taken effect, a substantial proportion could repeat some of the criticisms made by the formal opponents of the plan. The results were negative with respect to this hypothesis. Eighty-six per cent in the county and 96 per cent in the city were unable or unwilling to specify what they disliked in the plan. The responses in the county scatter among six specific responses: the cost in taxes, the loss of local control, too much power to the district, creation of an extra layer of government, more opportunity for corruption in politics, and the statement that the respondent was satisfied with things and had nothing to gain. These responses are relatively sensible, in light of the issue—that is, they reflect formal argument among experts and publicists. *However,* no more than 5 per cent of the involved, heavy-voting suburban sample named any one of them. Thus of the 60 per cent in the suburban sample who said they had voted, only one in five could—at the most generous estimate—have responded with any specific dislike of the District Plan.

The Future of Metropolitan Government Plans

In the wake of the massive defeat suffered by the District Plan, there were several responses by civic notables. One group reaffirmed its intention of trying for "all-out merger of city and county." [4] Another spoke of using whatever piecemeal tactics were available within the given framework of local government to effect changes recommended by the Metropolitan St. Louis Survey's public reports. Among many leaders there was a general belief that the overwhelming defeat of the plan made any further effort completely hopeless. At the end of the interview we asked our respondents what they thought of the business in general.

"Do you think the St. Louis city-county area needs action of this sort in the future? Do we need closer city-county cooperation?" Such a question is admittedly vague; however, it rings the chord of integrating the halves of the metropolis. The results were overwhelmingly

[4] They did so in 1962 and were even more soundly defeated.

"yes" in the suburbs: 68 per cent said "yes," 19 per cent "no," and the remainder had no opinion. In the city, comparable figures were: 53 per cent "yes" and 7 per cent "no." *Thus the general sentiment for areawide cooperation remains about as strong as it was in 1957.*

When we asked those who thought such action was needed "Why do you say that?" they answered in the terms shown in Table 6–15.

Table 6-15. Reasons Given for Believing Closer Cooperation Is Needed

Reason	Percentage Mentioning in:	
	City	County
1. Would promote progress, expansion, growth	11	15
2. Would improve services of local government	10	13
3. Would make for uniformity, more order, more equity	7	10
4. Would be more efficient in general	3	9
5. Would help improve, bolster up, the central city	5	4
6. Would equalize costs among the areas	4	3
7. Would be cheaper all around	4	2
8. All others	7	11
9. Cooperation not needed	7	19
10. No information	42	15
	100	101
	(81)	(165)

Half the city sample and nearly two-thirds of the suburbanites could give specific reasons why they support further action along the lines of the District Plan. This is indeed striking. Furthermore, it is notable that dissatisfaction with service levels does not appear very important in this tally. Such matters as economic development for the area, order, equity, and efficiency loom much larger than simple improvement of services.

Here are some of the responses.

Question. Do you think the St. Louis city-county area needs (more) action of this sort in the future? Do we need closer city-county cooperation? Why do you say that?

Yes. The main point is traffic and similar administration in all communities. Laws should be uniform. Enforcement should be uniform, not one rule in Clayton, another in Richmond Heights (suburban).

Yes. For one thing there are a lot of people in the county that are always fighting about who pays what taxes, and I feel that the county people benefit from our police department and hospitals and pay no taxes for the services. If there was cooperation then the tax on services such as police, hospitals, and such would be equally divided. Now the county people use our hospital on Arsenal Street and don't pay the taxes on it, and the police department goes over the county line if necessary and the county doesn't pay for that either (central city).

Yes. So it could be one big government and only pay one layer of salaries. St. Louis has not expanded in over 100 years, and if they don't do something about it soon it will be a ghost city. All they do is make it easier for the people who live 35 or 40 miles away to come here and make money and take it back out there to spend. The city is going down residentially and the people are all coming into St. Louis to work so why not get together and make one big city like other places do? (central city).

No. Webster is a nice community as it is. We pay higher taxes here, but we have a good government set-up here and I don't think it would benefit Webster to combine with another government (suburban).

The arguments given for further action are those used by the proponents of the District Plan. Let us see what reasons are given by those opposing further action. Of the 19 per cent in the suburbs who said nothing is needed, 9 per cent simply said they were satisfied with things as they are; 4 per cent said "each to his own, city and county." The other responses were scattered: very few persons mentioned taxes or additional cost.

Thus it might appear that the population, particularly the suburban population, is for metropolitan government in general. (Much more so in general than in particular.) When specific action is urged, it is clear that the response will change: though our respondents were not particularly coherent about what they objected to in change, the fact remains that an overwhelming majority of voters had voted against the plan— and those who didn't were heavily opposed to it. What, then, do the respondents think they would like, in the way of further metropolitan cooperation?

Table 6-16. What Sort of Plan Respondents Would Favor Next Time Around

Type of Plan	Percentage Mentioning in:	
	City	County
1. Merger	12	19
2. Arrangement stronger than district	5	12
3. Same: the District Plan	4	7
4. Arrangement weaker than district	8	6
5. Consolidation of municipalities in the county	—	5
6. All others	7	7
7. Don't Know	19	15
8. No information, irrelevant	46	28
	101	99
	(81)	(165)

Only 35 per cent in the city and 57 per cent in the county knew what they wanted. Of those who did, however, a clear majority wanted a plan stronger than the District Plan. Thirty-one per cent in the suburbs and 17 per cent in the city favored such a plan; only 11 per cent in the suburbs and 8 per cent in the city favored weaker solutions. The public for metropolitan government in the area feels at least an aesthetic attraction to a strong areawide government. By implication, the District Plan lost because of weakness: yet we do not know how this was defined, given the ignorance of the plan that was current among our respondents.

Here are some of their (rather vague) ideas on a desirable future plan.

Question. What kind of a plan would you favor next time?

A plan where everybody was satisfied by the whole deal. A plan that would help the taxpayer instead of the politician.

A plan giving the board less power and the people more power.

One covered by each township in the county and one from each ward in the city and to be selected by popular vote.

I don't know about city-county cooperation, but I think the county ought to go together in bigger groups. There are too many little ones, like this Marvin Terrace is only a couple of blocks.

A well-studied, well-coordinated, overall, complete, aggressive plan. I do not believe that half a loaf is better than none.

Complete thorough consolidation. I don't know how to explain it, but in my mind, it has to be thorough. In other words, eliminate all our services here—fire, police, everything—and put it all under one rule.

I think the city was giving its way to the county the way the plan was drawn up. I want the government of the city to run itself and the government of the county to run itself, only cooperate in traffic and law enforcement, but I don't think it should go any further than that. They should set a metropolitan traffic and law enforcement group. These men worked for years to draw up this plan and you want me to tell you in a few minutes what I want. I don't know what I want, I just don't like this one due to the higher taxes.

One government for the entire area. A complete merger with one municipal government. I'm somewhat of an idealist, and the main reason I voted against the District Plan is that I think the merger is better and I felt that if the District Plan were voted in I'd never get a chance to vote for a merger. We wouldn't gain anything on the District Plan. As I mentioned before, as far as I could tell, none of these individual districts would have any authority. They would formulate a plan and suggest it. For example, a freeway type street running from the city to the county connecting with state routes. They could plan the location of the route. Then they would have to bring this before various municipalities through which the route passed and ask them if they would please put the route through. And, if the municipality said "no, we don't want a route through" that would be the end of the plan because (they would have) no authority. In this case we would only have ten more people to deal with on all the problems.

Conversation, Opinion, and the Vote

In summary, the District Plan was an important aspect of the conversational ferment in the metropolitan area. Particularly in the suburbs, many persons reported having talked over the plan with one or more of their close friends, kin, work associates, or neighbors. The talk was preponderantly negative or mixed with respect to the plan. Few persons thought they learned from such talk; when they did, they either learned facts about the plan or learned how other people felt. Most of them believed that most of their friends who voted, voted against the plan.

Though they talked, and some learned, they did not really know much about the issue of the election. Only a minority of the voters could have been correctly informed on any aspect of the District Plan, among either electorate. Nevertheless, they defeated it overwhelmingly. However, if few knew the facts, many could give good points in the plan—vague as they were—and only a few volunteered their own arguments against it. This was complemented by a general friendliness to the notion of future efforts at metropolitan integration. And, of those who did want more action, the largest bloc indicated they would like a plan stronger than the District Plan.

Such are the gross outlines of public response to the campaign. Let us turn now to the behavior of specific kinds of voters.

7

Opponents and Proponents

at the Grass Roots

Opposition to metropolitan government has typically centered in the suburbs—the "escaping" residential enclaves. In the history of efforts to create such a government, in both the St. Louis area and in Cuyahoga County, the suburbs have always been the stumbling block. For this reason, planners of plans devised to "get something through" typically anticipate suburban resistance and attempt to forestall it. Furthermore, the resulting campaign tends to deprecate the city's resistance and to focus on the suburbs. This obviously occurred in St. Louis. Nor are these assumptions on the part of planners and campaigners altogether incorrect; even though the District Plan lost in each area, it was most heavily defeated in the suburbs. This was the major battleground, where most residents became involved—conversationally and otherwise —and where the largest proportion voted.[1]

For these reasons our analysis of the kinds of people who voted and inclined in different directions will concentrate on the suburban sample. As noted earlier in this discussion, this sample of 165 persons, drawn

[1] As noted earlier, this was not true of Cuyahoga County — there the charter was defeated more decisively in the city of Cleveland (58 per cent versus 52 per cent).

from a larger sample interviewed three years previously and biased towards a concentration of those who care about local politics, is not completely representative of the total. What we want, however, is to analyse the "core electorate" of the suburban population, in its response to a metropolitan government issue. For this purpose, the sample is appropriate. Almost all of them had heard about the District Plan; 60 per cent voted in the election; those who voted came close to the division of the vote produced by the referendum; those who did not vote, but "leaned," were very similar. We now ask about this sample: What kinds of people were pro, con, and neutral? what kinds voted and did not vote? Later we will approach the question: what were the mechanisms of communication and influence? How were they related to the ongoing, everyday organization of the suburban communities?

Background Characteristics

First we will turn to the relatively stable social characteristics of the citizens. Age, sex, occupation, education, and income do not change much over a period of three years, compared to such attributes as residence, associations, and the like. For this reason we have relegated them to the status of "background" rather than active and interactive variables. Also relatively fixed are such political background attributes as voting preference. We turn now to ask: how did the pros and the cons compare on these differentia?

Social Background and Position on the District Plan

In Table 7–1 we have compared certain basic categories with each other in their position on the plan: The male and female, young, middle-aged, and older, those with differing educational, occupational, and financial levels. In general, we can make a few statements with considerable confidence.

First, it is clear that those who were in favor of the plan were disproportionately made up of men. They were also better educated, came from households with higher incomes, and were most likely to come from families where the male breadwinner was a professional, owner, or manager. Indeed, in the latter category a *majority* of those with opinions favored the plan. (This was the only sub-category of which this was true). The opponents of the plan were more likely to be women, to be older (aged thirty or more), to have less formal education, to be lower white-collar workers or manual workers, and to have incomes below the median for the sample. It is important to note, however, that there was also substantial opposition in categories that were more favorable to the plan, for these were also categories with the highest proportions *taking an active position*. The "No Opinion" class declines as the "Pros" increase.

As for the related question of who cared enough to *vote* on the plan among those with opinions, there are important regularities. Men were much more likely to have voted than women; the middle-aged, more likely than the young or the old (and particularly the young). But when we turn to the various measures of social rank, we find that the differences in participation do not hold. Between rich and poor, laborer and professional, college graduate and graduate of the eighth grade, the proportions did not vary significantly. This was very important for the electoral fate of the District Plan: the "good government supporters," who understood the morality play and applauded it, did not dominate the election. Those less involved with the norms of efficiency and growth turned out in disproportionate numbers for this particular election.[2] The only advantage accruing to the plan, through its differential appeal to the higher social ranks, was in the larger proportion with definite opinions among the better educated and those of professional, entrepreneurial, or managerial status.

We can hazard this interpretation. The District Plan, with its appeal to economic growth and fertility and its increased rationality of local government with better services as the final payoff, made sense to those familiar with the norms of economic efficiency and scale of operations.

[2] This finding is supported by Schmandt, *Reform in St. Louis*, page 52, Table 5. Taking townships by average social rank, there was *no* difference in turnout for the election.

Table 7-1. Opinion of the District Plan and Percentage Voting by Demographic Variables

	Opinion of Plan				%Voting	(N)*
	%Pro	%Neutral	%Con	%No Opinion		
Sex						
Female	14	11	48	27	44	90
Male	27	10	55	8	67	75
						165
Age						
50+	20	—	60	20	77	21
30–49	18	13	53	15	87	99
21–29	24	11	37	30	68	45
						165
Education						
To 8th	15	9	47	29	76	33
9–12th	15	13	50	21	77	89
12th+	40	7	50	4	79	43
						165
Occupation of Head of Household						
Blue-collar	12	14	56	19	73	57
Lower white-collar	9	9	61	21	75	23
Upper white-collar	42	9	37	12	80	43
						126
Gross Household Income						
Below median	14	7	62	17	74	71
Above median	26	13	43	17	74	76
						147

* Numbers vary for occupation and income of household due to lack of response on these questions.

They could discount the increase in taxes, for this was relatively minor (and they were more likely to have high incomes). But for the less educated, the wage workers, the poor, the increase of taxes implicit in the plan both stimulated a vote and drowned out the advantages promised by its sponsors.

Political Background

Political background factors were derived from the 1957 sample survey of opinions and participation. The stability of such matters over time is not known, but it is plausible to assume that, for most persons most of the time, such things as party preference and orientation to campaigns remain pretty constant. Less certain, however, are such matters as preference in metropolitan government. In this section we shall note the relationships between each of these and position on the District Plan of 1959.

Voting Habits. The opponents of the plan were most likely to be Democratic or to express no preference between the parties: the supporters were overwhelmingly Republican. Of those who voted against the plan, 33 per cent were Democratic, 42 per cent "independent," and only 25 per cent Republican. Of those who voted for, the percentages were 22, 22, and 56. Or, combining by their preferences, those who voted and those who did not, we have the distribution by political affiliation shown in Table 7–2.

Table 7-2. Party Preference and Position on the District Plan (by Percentage)

Party Preference	Position on Plan			
	Pro	Neutral	Con	No Opinion or Not Ascertained
Democratic (64)	13	9	42	36
Independent (no preference) (47)	13	4	60	23
Republican (53)	36	17	41	6

The Republicans were substantially more friendly towards the plan than either of the other two categories. They were also more likely to have voted in the election than were the Democrats—57 per cent compared with 42 per cent. It is surprising, however, to find that the large proportion of Independents voted. Usually persons with no party preference fall somewhere between the two parties in propensity to vote. In this election, however, 70 per cent so designating themselves voted. As is evident, they were the most overwhelmingly *opposed* of any category. Rejection of party does not necessarily mean acceptance of nonpartisan reform.

Respondents were also asked which was most important in helping them make up their minds in local elections: talking with people or media such as television, radio, and the newspapers. There were differences by voting or not voting: of those who voted, 23 per cent said the mass media were most important. Of those who abstained, 34 per cent said this. This is tentative evidence that the active electorate in the suburbs is more likely to be people-oriented in its political communication. (We will return to this theme later.) Nevertheless, there is no difference, by orientation towards the media or people, between supporters and opponents of the District Plan.

Earlier Opinions. In 1957, these same respondents were asked to evaluate the various possible changes in the St. Louis city-county governmental structure, including "no change." The alternatives included merger, reentry of the city into St. Louis County, a "federal system" (something like the District Plan), the consolidation of the county municipalities, or simply doing nothing at all. This resurvey allowed us to test the constancy of opinions given three years earlier, before the metropolitan government was even a public issue. In the 1957 interview the respondent was first asked which of the alternatives he liked best.

Though these are very small samples, certain things are clear. First, preferences (1957) for the federal system, which was very much like the District Plan, had no predictive value for 1959. Second, aside from the federal system, those preferring *any* kind of change ran to very similar opinions of the District Plan—about two to one against it. Third, the statement in 1957 that one preferred *no change* was highly pre-

Table 7-3. 1957 Preference by Position on the District Plan (by Percentage)

| | Position on Plan: | | | | |
1957 Preference	Pro	Neutral	Con	No Opinion	Total
1. Merger	24	13	43	20	100 (46)
2. One county	30	4	57	8	99 (23)
3. Federal system	13	8	60	20	101 (24)
4. Consolidation	30	15	50	5	100 (27)
5. Status quo	7	13	55	25	100 (40)
6. No opinion	20	—	40	40	100 (5)
					(165)

dictive of response to the District Plan: of those with definite opinions, eight-ninths opposed the District Plan. The same distribution is apparent when we consider only those who voted. Of those favoring merger who voted, 9 supported the plan and 7 opposed: of those favoring the *status quo* who voted, 1 supported the plan and 17 opposed. Forty per cent of the plan's support among voters came from those who most wanted merger.

Similar results obtain when we consider another question asked in 1957: Which change would you most *dislike?* Of those who most disliked merger, and voted, 33 voted against the plan and 5 supported it. Of those who most disliked "leaving things alone," 11 supported the plan and 19 opposed it. Adding to those who disliked merger those who disliked "one big county," of 45 persons voting, 89 per cent voted against the District Plan.

In summary, two conclusions can be drawn from comparing 1957 opinions on metropolitan government with 1959 opinions. First, those who said they preferred to leave things alone in 1957 were overwhelmingly opposed to the metropolitan plan of 1959. Second, the strongest support for the plan was among those who had been identified as supporters of outright merger in 1957. Thus one might hazard the proposition: regardless of the kind and degree of metropolitan government proposed, it will be fought by those who like the *status quo* and it will be supported by those who want the extreme of integration-merger. The quandary of those who campaign for metropolitan government is clear: they can mobilize their support only by emphasizing the very aspect of the plan most detestable to their opposition. In fact, they will mobilize their own opposition. They cannot possible satisfy, or mollify, both factions at once. The moderate plan does not placate the "stand-patters," but it probably decreases support among those who prefer outright merger.

Exposure to the Campaign

We turn now to the differential impact of the campaign upon the proponents and opponents of the District Plan. Here we wish to find how they differ, if they differ, on such matters as: (1) perception of the leadership structure pro and con; (2) awareness of the different media and their positions on the issue; (3) competence with respect to what was in the District Plan; (4) what they heard in political conversation; and (5) how they thought their friends probably voted on the issue.

Leadership. Of those who were favorable to the District Plan (33), only 2 persons (or 6 per cent) could name one leader in their locality who supported it. Of those who opposed, 6 persons (or 7 per cent) could name one. However, 14 per cent of those who opposed the plan named a local leader *opposed,* as did 12 per cent of the plan's supporters. Thus the evidence, scanty as it is, would suggest that twice as many local leaders in opposition got through.

As we have noted earlier, very few metropolitan area leaders were named at all, with one major exception—Raymond Tucker, the Mayor of the City of St. Louis. He was known to almost all the suburban sample, and a majority knew his position on the issue. Of our sample, the percentages recognizing his stand were as shown in Table 7–4. A majority, regardless of position on the plan, knew that Tucker opposed. (Only those with no opinion were generally uninformed.) The majority is larger for those who opposed the plan, however, than for

Table 7-4. Tucker's Position as Seen by Proponents and Opponents of the Plan (in Percentages)

Tucker's Position:	Position on Plan			
	Pro	Neutral	Con	No Opinion
1. Con (accurate)	54	61	66	23
2. Pro (inaccurate)	21	22	17	13
3. Don't Know	25	17	18	64
	100	100	101	100

those who supported it. The latter were quite likely either to say Tucker was in favor or to say they didn't know his position.

The importance of Tucker's opposition is clear from two additional items. First, Tucker is by far the most trusted leader in the city-county area who was involved in the campaign. Of those who responded to the question "Which of these is the most trustworthy?" some 80 per cent among both proponents and opponents designated Tucker. Furthermore, Tucker's reputation includes, among other attributes, that of expertise. He has a major technical achievement in the past—solution of the St. Louis smog problems while he was smoke abatement officer—and he is a professional technician by training (an engineer). When the different opinion classes are compared with respect to the reasons they impute to Tucker for his stand, the major reasons given are "the judgment of an expert." Specifically, respondents said "He considered the District Plan to be inadequate," or "He wanted another type of plan." Thirty-one per cent of the opponents gave these reasons, and 21 per cent of the proponents did so. Of those who were neutral on the plan, 45 per cent mentioned these reasons. Tucker's opposition to the plan carried a weight of technical authority which probably cancelled out much of the argument for the plan, since it was largely technical in nature. There is, thus, good evidence to support the contention that Tucker's opposition was a strong blow to the chances of the District Plan.

Some evidence of the channels through which Tucker's opinions were carried is contained in the ways in which they heard about his position.

We have noted that proponents are Republicans; they are also, evidently, "newspaper voters"—at least, they rely much less upon television than do the opponents.

Table 7-5. Source of Knowledge Concerning Tucker's Position (in Percentages)

Source	Respondent's Position on Plan:			
	Pro	Neutral	Con	No Opinion
1. Newspapers	64	44	37	17
2. Television	12	33	37	10
3. Other	5	—	—	—
4. Don't Know Position	20	22	25	73
	100	99	99	100

The Media. We turn now to the media which carried the campaign. We have noted three major channels—the *Post-Dispatch*, the local community press, and the local television stations. How many persons, among the proponents, opponents, and neutrals, recognized the correct positions of each of these?

It will be recalled that the *Post* was committed to an "all-out campaign for the District Plan"; the community press was overwhelmingly and noisily opposed; the local television output was mixed, and the stations themselves neutral (with the exception of one which editorialized for the plan a few days before elections). Thus we have an opportunity of seeing (1) how many knew at all, (2) how many "knew" wrong, and (3) how this varied by position.

First, for the committed media, it is clear that a voter was most apt to think he knew the position of the medium on "his own side." Only 62 per cent of the opposition knew the *Post's* position, compared with 76 per cent of the proponents; on the other hand, 54 per cent of the opposition knew the community press' position, compared with only 27 per cent of those who favored the plan. Turning now to correctness of this "knowledge," it is clear that it follows the same pattern. Of those who were personally against the plan, only 46 per cent were accurate

Table 7-6. Positions of the Media, by Position on District Plan (in Percentages)

Medium and Position Imputed	Respondent's Position on Plan:			
	Pro	Neutral	Con	No Opinion
1. *Post-Dispatch*				
Pro (accurate)	67	56	46	17
Neutral (inaccurate)	6	6	13	—
Con (inaccurate)	3	—	2	3
Don't Know	24	39	38	80
	100	101	99	100
2. Local Community Press				
Pro (inaccurate)	—	6	5	3
Neutral (inaccurate)	3	12	5	—
Con (accurate)	24	39	44	13
Don't Know	73	44	46	83
	100	101	100	99
3. Television				
Pro (inaccurate)	6	33	10	7
Neutral (accurate)	48	33	60	13
Con (inaccurate)	—	—	2	—
Don't Know	46	33	28	80
	100	99	100	100

concerning the position of the *Post-Dispatch*. But of those who were for the plan, 67 per cent were accurate. The same regularities hold with the local community press. It was opposed and, of the respondents who also opposed the plan, 44 per cent were accurate in stating this—compared to only 24 per cent of those who favored the plan. It is interesting to note that those who were neutral or had mixed feelings about the plan were in between the two committed positions in their accuracy.

As for television, it is apparent that most opponents and neutrals thought they knew what the stations' positions were—but supporters tended to say they did not know. (It will be recalled that supporters were not nearly so likely to have learned important information via television). A curious item here is the tendency for neutrals to believe the television stations had been favorable to the plan; this is consistent with some estimates by the committed. For, if they imputed a position to the stations, they tended to say they *were* pro-plan.

We have been making very minimal assumptions. We have assumed that respondents with positions perceived the media with some distortion, tending to believe that it coincided with their own position. It is also worth keeping in mind, however, that the proponents and opponents were very likely oriented to different media—and exposure to the media may very well have influenced their own position. We will return to this hypothesis later.

Competence and Position on the Plan. We have discussed the three major aspects of the District Plan which its proponents struggled to communicate to the public. These included tax rate, governance and effects on existing governments, and services to be provided. As a crude test of the relationship between knowledge and position on the plan, we have separated the respondents into those who were accurate on none of these points, on one only, or on two or more.

Table 7-7. Knowledge of Plan and Position on the Plan (in Percentages)

Aspects Correctly Known	Position on the Plan			
	Pro	Neutral	Con	No Opinion
None	12	17	23	80
One	49	50	50	20
Two or More	39	33	27	—
	100	100	100	100
	(33)	(18)	(84)	(30)

The proponents are better informed about the provisions of the District Plan; even so, over 60 per cent of the proponents knew at most only one major provision of the plan, compared to 73 per cent of the opponents. Whether knowledge increased the likelihood of favoring the plan or whether a position favoring the plan increased knowledge is difficult to determine with our data. We can say, however, that those who knew nothing about the plan, but voted, voted 14 to 1 against; those who knew one item voted 3 to 1 against; those who knew two or more items voted slightly less than 2 to 1 against. Opposition varied by knowledge. Still, it must be noted that even the relatively well informed defeated the plan decisively.

Table 7-8. Political Conversations with Kinfolk, Friends, Neighbors, and Work Associates among Those with Positions on the Plan (in Percentages)

Conversations with:	Position on the District Plan:		
	Pro	Neutral	Con
A. Kinfolk			
Mostly pro	24	6	1
Mixed	36	17	23
Mostly con	3	11	35
None	46	67	42
B. Friends			
Mostly pro	00	00	00
Mixed	30	11	24
Mostly con	00	6	19
None	70	83	57
C. Neighbors			
Mostly pro	3	6	2
Mixed	9	6	10
Mostly con	6	6	25
None	83	82	63
D. Work Associates			
Mostly pro	3	12	2
Mixed	18	12	15
Mostly con	18	25	25
None	61	50	59
Total Number	(33)	(18)	(84)

The Conversational Ferment. A very important aspect of this campaign was the casual discussion of the plan among kinfolk, friends, neighbors, and work associates. It is important to see how the proponents and the opponents differed, if they differed, in the messages they heard through these channels. We shall consider, at this point, conversations and their dominant tones. The committed, those with definite and consistent positive or negative positions, were more likely to have been in conversations about the plan. Those opposed to the plan were somewhat more apt to have done so than those who supported it—especially with their friends and their neighbors. The conversations were more apt to be favorable to the plan, or "mixed" for those who supported it; they were more apt to be unfriendly to the plan among the opponents. Though the samples are small, the latter proposition is very strongly supported: for each category of relationship, the opponents of the plan were much more likely to report that the conversations in which they had been involved were mostly unfriendly to the plan.

We turn now to the respondent's estimate of how his friends voted on the plan. Here again, there is considerable variation by position. First, with respect to how many they thought voted, the opponents of the plan were more likely to think that *most* of their friends had voted. Those with positions were most likely to make some estimate of their friends' turnout; the neutrals or persons with mixed opinions, next most likely; those with no opinion were least likely to give an estimate. As for the direction of their friends' vote, they tended to see them voting as they did.

Table 7-9. How Many of Your Friends Do You Think Voted in the Election: (in Percentages)

Estimate	Position on Plan:			
	Pro	Neutral	Con	No Opinion
Most of them	36	11	54	3
Some of them	33	35	14	20
Don't know	30	44	32	77
	99	90	100	100
	(33)	(18)	(84)	(46)

Table 7-10. Direction of Friends' Vote by Position on Plan (in Percentages)

Position	Position on Plan:			
	Pro	Neutral	Con	No Opinion
Mostly Pro	12	6	1	3
Mixed	30	28	8	7
Mostly Con	27	22	58	13
Don't Know	32	44	32	77
	101	100	99	100
	(33)	(18)	(84)	(46)

The variations by position on the plan are very regular; yet even the supporters of the plan rarely believed that most of their friends voted for it. On the other hand, the opponents were overwhelmingly convinced that their friends voted mostly against it. Both the conversational ferment and the network of friendship seem to have worked against the District Plan.

Social Structure and the Political Communication

We have been discussing the variations in position on the District Plan as they relate to the respondent's exposure to the campaign. Now it is important to look at the relationship between the respondent's social position and what he heard, to see if his social position affected what he heard and therefore his opinions and actions. By social position we refer to one's everyday role in the suburban associational system—in the concentric worlds of the municipality, the residential community (or local area), the neighborhood. In approaching this problem, we will use a simple typology developed elsewhere.[3] It allows us to classify

[3] See Scott Greer, "The Social Structure and Political Process of Suburbia, An Empirical Test," *Rural Sociology, op. cit.* for a detailed presentation of the way the typology was developed and of its empirical power. We have simplified the typology still further by combining the "deviant" cases with the Community Actors.

persons by their degree of involvement in the spatially defined organizations of suburbia.

There are three types of "actors," or participators. These are (1) the Isolates, who do not neighbor, do not read the local community paper for local news, and do not belong to any local voluntary organizations: (2) the Neighbors, who do not belong to organizations, but participate vigorously in the small world of the neighborhood, and (3) the Community Actors, who are the members of the local voluntary organizations. In this sample, which is biased towards participation in local political affairs, we have maximized the proportion of Community Actors: they are 53 per cent of the total, compared with 17 per cent Neighbors and 30 per cent Isolates.

Using the data collected in 1957 for our respondents, we classified them in this manner. As a demonstration of the utility of these constructs, we have analyzed the relationship between them and a brief, five-point scale of participation in local political affairs. In Table 7–11 we indicate the results. We have combined the first two steps of the

Table 7-11. Participational Types and Political Types (in Percentages)

| Political Type | Participational Type: | | |
	Isolates	Neighbors	Community Actors
Type I	62	39	29
Type II	38	61	71
	100	100	100

scale—those who do not participate at all and those who only vote—and they are compared with the last three steps—those who take sides, attempt to persuade others, and attend public meetings.[3] In general,

[3] The scale is a Guttman-type, ordinal scale. That is, people who attend meetings do all of the other things; those who try to persuade others but do not attend meetings will still take sides and vote. Those who take sides will also vote. The nature of the scale and its application to a larger sample are presented in "The Mass Society and the Parapolitical Structure," (with Peter Orleans) *American Sociological Review*, Vol. 27, No. 5, pp. 634–646.

Type I refers to those whose maximal political activity is the ritual of the vote; Type II refers to those whose participation in local politics goes beyond simply voting.

Thus our participational types relate (1) the everyday organizational and associational structure of the suburban neighbors and (2) the political processes.

The tables above refers only to data collected in the sample survey of 1957. We shall use these tools to analyze the referendum of 1959. First, however, it is important to describe the makeup of the classes of participators. Otherwise they might seem to be simply disguises of other, simpler variables.

1. *Occupation*: Community Actors are most apt to be in the white-collar occupations (63 per cent), followed by Isolates (52 per cent), and Neighbors (21 per cent).

2. *Education*: Community Actors are most highly educated (16 per cent grade school, compared with 32 per cent college and 52 per cent high school), followed by Isolates (26, 22, and 52 per cent respectively) and Neighbors (23, 14, and 63 per cent).

3. *Age differences*: The Community Actors are more likely to include persons in the age range of highest civic and political activity—35 to 54 years old. Seventy per cent of them are this age, compared with 58 per cent of the Isolates and 36 per cent of the Neighbors. Both Isolates and Neighbors include more older persons (around 30 per cent compared with 15) than the Community Actors, and Neighbors include more younger adults (35, compared with about 15 per cent for each of the other types).

4. *Sex differences*: There is no significant difference between Isolates and Neighbors; each is 60 per cent female. Community Actors are somewhat more likely to be male (50 per cent).

Though there are differences between the three participational types on each of these background factors, these differences do not determine the variations in political behavior. For one thing, Isolates and Community Actors are the most alike; yet their political behavior is the most different. For another, the differences in background noted are not adequate to account for the differences in political behavior. Finally, other research has shown that Community Actors with low education are politically more competent than Isolates with college degrees.

Indeed, we may think of background characteristics as selective—helping determine who will adopt one or the other of these modes of relating to the social environment. Once a person has adopted a mode, however—involvement in neighboring, participation in the community —the aspects of his role become powerful predictors of his behavior. The behavior in which we are most interested is response to the issue of metropolitan government in the referendum of 1959. Let us see if these measures, based on information collected in 1957, about these same respondents, will allow us to explain some of the responses to the referendum.

Social Type, Involvement, and Competence. A useful way of categorizing responses to the election is to trichotomize: some persons voted in the referendum, others had definite opinions about it, and still others had no opinion at all. Let us see how this varied by our social participational types.

Table 7-12. Social Type and Response to the Referendum (by Percentages)

Response	Social Type:		
	Isolates	Neighbors	Community Actors
No Opinion	20	25	15
Opinion But Didn't Vote	40	32	18
Voted	40	43	67
	100	100	100

It is clear that voting increases as we move from Isolates to Community Actors. It is also apparent that Neighbors behave more nearly like Isolates than like the latter. A very interesting aspect of the table, however, is the shifting proportion with opinions who did not vote (40, 32, and 18 per cent). Put another way, of those with opinions, *50 per cent* of the Isolates voted, *60 per cent* of the Neighbors, and *79 per cent* of the Community Actors. It is clear that opinion formation does not vary much between the three types, but activation does. This we would explain as a result of involvement in the nonpolitical, but politically relevant, social system of the suburban community, or what has been termed the parapolitical system.

Personal knowledge about the District Plan was not commonplace. One would not learn much that was accurate and important from social interaction—indeed, the daily newspapers were the major sources of such information. Therefore we do not expect very close relationships between the types and knowledge of the plan. Indeed, the relationship

Table 7-13. Social Type and Knowledge of the District Plan

Number of Provisions Accurately Known	Social Type:		
	Isolate	Neighbor	Community Actor
None	42	25	25
One	32	54	47
Two or More	26	21	28
	100	100	100

is not striking. Neighbors are more likely to know one provision and least likely to know two or more; Isolates are most apt to know none of the provisions, but there is little difference between the latter and the Community Actors as far as knowing two or more important provisions.

This is related to another finding. Although Community Actors were much more likely to vote than were the other two categories, this does not mean they differed significantly in the direction of their vote. In fact, about 25 per cent of each type who voted, voted for the District Plan. It was beaten by three to one in each category.

The Channels of Communication

The greater involvement of the Community Actors leads us to consider their conversational interaction with respect to the District Plan.

Table 7-14. Social Type and Conversation on the District Plan

Conversation in Given Relationships	Social Type:		
	Isolate	Neighbor	Community Actor
1. Relatives	42	32	56
2. Neighbors	17	29	32
3. Co-Workers	36	25	36
4. Friends	20	43	32

Since they have more of a stake in politics, we would expect them to have been involved in more conversations with respect to the plan. With neighbors and with relatives, Community Actors are more likely to report conversations about the District Plan. However, this is not nearly so clear when co-workers and other friends are involved. Most striking, however, is the fact that 56 per cent of the Community Actors had been in conversation about the plan with their relatives. Interest in the issue may have been, so to speak, filtered through social constraint—conversations emerging only where it was safe to discuss such a topic.

We have suggested earlier that conversation was not so much a channel of information as of influence. We are in a position to make a suggestive check of the latter part of this hypothesis. Were people affected by the general tone and position of the media they used and the people with whom they talked? In approaching the question, we first divided our respondents. There were those who had said in the 1957 survey that they found people more helpful than media such as newspapers, television, and the radio, in making up their minds about local elections. One hundred and four of our respondents were in this category while forty-one had opted for the media. These preferences were related to social type. Briefly, 38 per cent of Isolates, 26 per cent of Neighbors, and only 21 per cent of the Community Actors preferred media to people as opinion referents. For those who were oriented to people we used the general tenor of the conversations (were they usually for, against, or mixed, on the plan?) in an effort to predict the respondent's position.

Table 7-15. The Tone of Conversations and Position on the District Plan

Conversation Content	Position on the Plan:	
	Pro or Neutral	Con
A. With Kin (49)		
Pro or Mixed	14	11
Con	3	21
B. With Friends (33)		
Pro or Mixed	8	14
Con	1	10
C. With Neighbors (30)		
Pro or Mixed	6	6
Con	3	15
D. With Co-Workers (37)		
Pro or Mixed	9	9
Con	8	11

The size of the samples does not justify even percentages. It is clear, however, that the relationships are consistent. They are arranged in declining order: the correlation between conversation content in the family and position on the plan is very strong, that between content of conversations with work associates and position is negligible.

It is, of course, possible that people simply perceived conversations to be roughly in line with their own opinions. Here, however, the variation among the relationships—particularly the contrast between the effects of conversations with kin and with work associates—would suggest that the conversations are reported independently of distortion. We would suggest, on the basis of these data, that the tone of the conversations among kin, friends, and neighbors was a very important element in the definition of positions on the District Plan issue.

We turn now to the 41 persons who said they relied mostly on the media in making up their minds about local elections. We have already noted that such persons were most apt to be Isolates, least apt to be Community Actors. We have used a further question from the 1957 survey: "Which of these (media) is most helpful to you in making up your mind?" This was a means of determining orientation. The numbers are too small to dignify with percentages; let it suffice to say that of 11 Isolates, 7 were oriented to the metropolitan media, 4 to the community press; of 10 Community Actors, 7 were oriented to the community press.

We have had to disregard the variation by social type and combine them in order to salvage enough cases to make any sense. When we dichotomize by media of orientation (losing 17 cases who did not express a clear preference in media) the results in Table 7–16 are obtained.

Table 7-16. Media of Orientation and Position on the Plan

Medium	Position on the Plan	
	Pro or Mixed	Con
Metropolitan	9	2
Community Press	4	9

Small as the sample is, this remains an extremely sharp and suggestive break. Those persons who are media-oriented with respect to local politics look to the metropolitan dailies if they are Isolates, the community press if they are Community Actors. Their media orientation, in turn, appears to have a real influence on their political positions with respect to metropolitan government.

Ideology after the Election

An election of any sort polarizes the population. From the middle ground, voters move towards the two poles; as they do so, greater heat (and less light) is generated, and the norms of exclusion begin to operate. The enemy is defined in terms of enmity only. It is therefore important to see how the persons supporting, opposing, and neutral with respect to the district plan defined the voters of their own and the other side. We have noted earlier that imputations of self-interest, corruption, and political irresponsibility were not very common. However, when we partial by the respondent's position we find them significantly concentrated. Each of the two poles defines the other side as basically immoral and itself as respectable. To the supporters of the plan, opponents are uninformed, corrupt, and politically irresponsible: supporters are informed and civic-minded. To the plan's enemies, its supporters are, again, uninformed, corrupt, self-interested; its opponents are property owners, self-respecting people who see no need for change. Those who were *neutral*, however, put the best face on the matter for both sides.

Table 7-17. Images of Voters for and against by Position on the Plan (by Percentages)

What Kind of Voters Were:	Position on the Plan			
	Pro	Neutral	Con	No Opinion
A. For the Plan				
Uninformed, corrupt, self-interested	7	11	29	7
Informed, civic minded	57	56	11	3
All others	21	22	40	23
Don't Know	15	11	20	67
	100	100	100	100
B. Against the Plan				
Uninformed, vested interests, politically irresponsible	46	17	6	7
Wanted no change, property owners	30	56	47	13
All others	9	16	34	20
Don't Know	15	11	13	60
	100	100	100	100

The Future. It will be remembered that a very large majority of the respondents said they thought that the area needed more action of the sort represented by the District Plan. When they are classified by their opinions on the plan, however, there is considerable variation. Ninety-seven per cent of those favorable to the plan said "Yes," compared to 78 per cent of those in the middle and only 55 per cent of the plan's opponents. This variation continues when they give their reasons for thinking so. Sixty per cent of the Plan's supporters have a ready ideological answer; they want to increase services, improve organization in the area, and encourage economic progress. Only 39 per cent of the neutrals give these reasons, however, and 32 per cent of the opponents. In fact, 40 per cent of the opponents could give no reasons.

A similar variation occurs in the kind of plan the factions would support. Seventy-five per cent of those who supported the plan would like another, as strong or stronger, compared to 45 per cent of those in the middle and only 34 per cent of those who opposed the plan. Thus it seems unlikely that a very strong metropolitan government plan would capture much more support than did the District Plan, at least in the suburban neighborhoods of St. Louis County.

Table 7-18. Preferred Future Action by Position on Plan (in Percentages)

| | Position on Plan | | | |
Next Plan Should Be:	Pro	Neutral	Con	No Opinion
Merger	33	28	12	17
Stronger than the District Plan	15	6	17	—
The Same	27	11	5	—
Weaker than the District Plan	6	6	10	7
Consolidation of Municipalities	3	11	6	—
None	—	—	5	—
All Other	—	—	5	—
No Opinion	17	39	40	76
	101	101	100	100

This concludes our discussion of the sample survey of St. Louis County citizens, carried out in the month immediately following the referendum on the District Plan. It is evident that most voters had only a very vague notion as to what the Plan was about. This, however, was not because of the organized campaign against it: indeed, there is little indication that either campaign affected the citizens directly. Only Mayor Tucker's position was generally known and effective. For the most part, however, the mass media and the conversational ferment seem to have been the key channels of influence.

Political conversations are part of the ongoing, everyday round of life for many people. They occur in the neighborhoods, the home, and at work. They have most effect among relatives, least at work. There they seem to be a sort of parlor game at which anyone can play without regard to competence or consequence. The relationship between the general tone of the conversations and the position of the respondent is a regular one: those who have heard conversations generally favorable to the plan are more likely to support it or, at least, maintain an open mind. For them it is an issue. But for those who have heard nothing but unfavorable comment, the probabilities of their taking a hostile stand are very great indeed.

Though conversations seem to affect political position, they do not seem to involve much information. Their chief output is perhaps the communication of norms and the ordering of behavior towards the position common to the group. The groups, in turn, are not primarily political in nature: we have called them elsewhere "the parapolitical structure" of the society. Rooted in the nonpolitical world of everyday life, they are a crucial underpinning for the finding of opinion in a society such as ours. Those who participate widely in this parapolitical world, the Community Actors, are a self-selected elite with a very determinate influence upon our public fate—one out of all proportion to their numbers. The community is theirs, because they want it. They vote vigorously, but their thought, as the foregoing pages indicate, is not always formulated rigorously.

Some Comparative Data

Unfortunately, we cannot replicate these inquiries for the Dade County and Cuyahoga County campaigns. However, there are some data which indicate the comparability of the elections. For example, in Cuyahoga County, a little over a month before the election only 66 per cent of a sample remembered reading or hearing anything about the new charter.[4] Less than one-third of the voters were strongly interested in the charter, and only one-third would hazard a guess as to "the main thing the charter would do.' More than three-fourths could not name any of the reasons given by those favoring it; the same proportion was unable to give any arguments made by its opponents.

In Cleveland, also, newspapers were the most important single source of information. Of the two-thirds who had heard about the charter, 63 per cent remembered reading about it in the Cleveland press. Thus 42 per cent of those sampled had been "exposed" to the newspaper campaign. Only about 5 per cent had heard of it through the television programs, and another 5 per cent through talking with other people. (It must be remembered that the last month of the campaign still lay ahead; this is usually by far the most intense, and was, in St. Louis, the major part of the show.)

In the Dade County election for Metro, only 26 per cent of the voters bothered to come to the polls. That this did not reflect any unusual competing attractions is clear from surveys conducted *after* the campaign was over and the new government in office. As Beiler and Wood put it:

. . . one expects a thing as big as Metro to make an impression. When only 32 per cent say they have heard or read about a new county charter and had a sliver of a correct idea about it, while 13 per cent have a quite wrong idea about it, that sinking sensation returns. It was not only in the telephone poll that 64.5 per cent said they did not know of any big change in the county government in the last couple of years. The same question had produced the identical 64.5 per cent shrugging response when asked (in an earlier face-to-face survey).[5]

[4] *Voters' Thinking on the County Charter*, Cleveland, Ohio: Social Surveys Company, September, 1959. The following statistics are from this study, a telephone survey of 1,022 households chosen systematically from the telephone directory.

[5] Ross C. Beiler and Thomas J. Wood, "Metropolitan Politics of Greater Miami," paper delivered at Annual Meeting of Southern Political Science Association, November 7, 1958 (mimeographed), page 13.

In short, whether metropolitan government fails or succeeds does not appear to depend on the awareness and competence of the citizens developed through the campaign.

As we have seen in the intensive analysis of the St. Louis County sample, a political process does go on at the grass roots. People do care (whether or not they care enough to learn what they care about), and they evoke a multitude of norms (whether they are relevant or not). Yet the net effects of this process were a crushing defeat in St. Louis, an almost even stand-off in Cuyahoga and Dade, with defeat in the former and victory in the latter. What is going on here?

8

What Happened?

Standing back a little distance from the St. Louis campaign, one is struck by an essential absurdity in the performance. A few people, intensely involved, swam in a sea of concepts and phrases—notions about the good life, the good society, the concrete effects of changes in a charter, the means of persuasion, the Spirit of Laws. They interacted furiously, within their circle of friends and supporters and, through intermediaries, with their enemies. They met on the hustings before interested faces, in conflict or in cooperation. Their eyes were forever glued to the mass media (on the eve of the election, a leader for the campaign exulted in the television space donated by one station—they were to take over "Eye on St. Louis!")

Yet the voters hardly knew who they were. They didn't recognize the face, and if they did they didn't know which side the leader was on or why he was there. Most of the voters didn't even know what the District Plan was. In Cuyahoga and Dade Counties the voters were equally somnolent and indifferent to the charter and the issues of the campaign. There is little evidence that any of the furious activity of the protagonists made much difference to the voters. Nor did most of the opposition register: some of "The Big Mules" are known to a fair segment of the population, but on this issue most of them just didn't get through the noise of everyday life.

Yet the three elections had very different results. Although the St. Louis campaign seems naive and slipshod in its execution, it was essentially the same kind of performance as that which won in Dade County. Civic entrepreneurs there created a Charter Board made up of "men of good will"—not powerful politicians. There were no precinct activities. There were speeches, continuous appearances in the media, advertisements. And apparently, in Dade, it worked. Of the quarter of the voters who went to the polls a small majority voted for the metropolitan charter. In contrast, in Cuyahoga County where there was a history of near-miss on the issue, the massive support for the new charter included almost everybody who was a "star" of the media; the politicians were neutralized, the opposition only amounted to a half dozen men who spoke on invitation and a few Negro ward leaders. Yet in Cuyahoga County the charter was beaten—barely in the suburbs, decisively in the central city (where it had been successful in earlier campaigns). What were the relationships, if any, between the charter drafting and exertions of the campaign, on one hand, and the electoral results on the other?

In theory, the common political culture should tie the activities of the campaigners to the decision making of the electorate. The delegates in the constitutional assembly should represent the community's interests, in congruence and in conflict. The charter should, in turn, become an issue leading to the mobilization of the various political components of the metropolis. However, such an issue is defined as "nonpolitical" (or at least "nonpartisan"), and the regular party machinery does not operate. Instead, the leaders of the campaign organize themselves through the morality plays of reform; they must then persuade the voters in these terms. Outside the authority of party and the loyalty of national class groups, the individual voter is supposed to make up his mind on the issues—the validity of arguments and counterarguments, the image of the desirable city and how to produce it.

In fact, the morality play of metropolitan reform seems to have allowed the campaigns to organize only at the top. Within the rubrics of progress and fertility, better services and efficiency, the leaders could talk to each other and maintain a social group with cohesion, commitment, and labor. The morality also allowed them to ask and receive resources—thousands of dollars, free time on the media, free space in buildings. It also allowed the opposition to formulate a position, to organize *itself* against the new constitution, and to gather resources. Finally, the morality allowed opponents and proponents to talk to each other: it made possible the face-to-face debates and the indirect debates through the mass media.

Thus the campaigns proceeded behind a massive facade of rational thought and logical argument. Seldom have so many thorny problems, involving theoretical and empirical unknowns, been aired on the front page of the daily papers. Seldom have so many businessmen, lawyers, elected officials, politicians, administrators, and League ladies taken public stands on abstract and difficult issues. Seldom have so few worked so hard and succeeded in confusing so many.

For, at the grass roots, the voters did not know what was going on. This seems to be the most general way of stating the findings from the St. Louis panel study. And in Cuyahoga County, in Dade County, our evidence indicates that matters were much the same. A leader in the fight for Miami Metro says: "There's an underestimation of the composite judgment of the people. First, the campaign was so close to them they had the opportunity to get information and judge it. Second, the concept was so logical that it carried its own weight." But, as Beiler and Wood put it, "one gets that sinking feeling" when it is clear that two-thirds of the people had no notion of what Metro was about.

Voters and the Mass Media

Having no access to the ordinary party labels which divide the American electorate into moieties and structure its decision, the campaigners could only define the decision as "all or nothing." Having no party organization, they could only reach the voters through the mass media. However, many voting studies indicate the failure of the media

to decide an election during the brief period of a presidential campaign
—and how much briefer was that for the District Plan, the Cuyahoga
County Charter, the Dade County metropolitan government. The
media cannot be prime movers: they can only reinforce pre-existing
norms and activate the population to vote accordingly.[1]

The voters, however, had little background knowledge with which
to evaluate the plans as expressions of basic norms. Nor were the
morality plays clearly grasped and intensely felt. Instead, the average
voter was confused and only marginally involved. Though he might
recognize and approve of some aims expressed in the new charter, he
could not be certain it would indeed effect them. In such a situation,
he turned to the authoritative figures in the metropolitan area: in St.
Louis, he listened to Mayor Tucker. Tucker, however, was not an
effective force because of his organizational power or his personal,
face-to-face dynamism. Instead, Tucker was the face reflected on the
magic screen of the mass media. Like Truman in 1948, Tucker had
the enormous advantage of being a *news-making actor.*

Legend already has it that Truman, as he whistle-stopped across the
nation, took his own case to the people and won despite a hostile press. What
Truman actually did, it would seem, was to make "news." The press—or
magazines or radio—could editorialize against the administration; their presentation of the news that Truman was making could be more or less subtly
biased through headlines, spacing, choice of words, and the like. But since
what Mr. Truman said was news, his appeal to class interests commanded
attention and helped bring the strays back to the fold.[2]

The Tucker "image" had been created over many years by the
civic leaders and the press. He stood as a symbol of authoritative
judgment on local government, and his authority rested upon technical
expertise, "nonpolitical" commitments, the welfare of the community
as a whole. Thus his negative judgment of the District Plan, based
upon a technical analysis of its effects upon the City of St. Louis as

[1] See, for example, *The People's Choice, Voting,* and others of that kind.
[2] "The Mass Media and Voting," Kurt and Gladys Engel Lang, in *American Voting Behavior,* edited by Eugene Burdick and Arthur J. Brodbeck, Glencoe: The Free Press, 1959, page 224.

well as the metropolitan area as a whole, was one of the few messages that penetrated the fog of uncertainty.

As for the voters, they were struggling with morality plays which they did not clearly understand. The removal of the Purification Ritual from the triad (Purification, Progress, Fertility) left the sub-plot— "keep our local officials in office and our municipalities as they are"— in violent conflict with the main plot—"improve our government by radical reorganization, for we are in bad shape." In St. Louis the result was a vicious attack on the plan by the upholders of the *status quo,* who could not be attacked in terms of the conventional plot; the same thing occurred in Cuyahoga County.

Indeed, the District Plan itself was vulnerable to the conventional charges of corruption. It seemed to support the local political *status quo* and it actually called for more taxes, presumably to be spent by the "dirty politicians." And the effort to use the fertility theme as a counterargument seems to have fallen quite flat. Where it was noted by the respondents in the panel survey, they tended to nominate it as the "phoniest" argument. Many could see that (1) no politicians would lose their jobs and (2) taxes would be raised. This, then, invalidated the progress and efficiency theme.

The opposition undoubtedly had one important effect. It forced the endless complication of the issue through challenge, rebuttal, re-rebuttal, and so on until election time. The sheer complication undoubtedly had a deleterious effect on the chances of the plan. Then the educational television programs showing the Board of Freeholders at work and the debates over the District Plan must have further complicated the issue. We are not suggesting that such complication is unsuitable to the subject; however, it does not seem to be an effective way of creating support for radical innovation. (As one leader said, "usually people want a bond issue *explained.*") In fact, the endless emphasis on complexity probably helped destroy trust—in the plan, its sponsors, the voter's own judgment, perhaps even the antagonists.

The mass media, by the way in which they structure and present political reality, may contribute to a widespread and chronic distrust of political life. ... The mass media tend to emphasize crisis and stress it in lieu of normal processes of decision-making. Such distrust has its roots in the complexity of events and of problems in which the mass audience is involved.[3]

The emphasis on conflict and complexity may have discouraged many people who were predisposed to favor metropolitan government.

Finally, as a result of the confusion and distrust created by the opposition and the debates, many voters took the traditional way out. Sixty per cent did not vote in St. Louis County; 80 per cent did not vote in the city. Sixty per cent did not vote in Cuyahoga County; 74 per cent did not vote in Dade County. The peasant adage "better the evil that is known" and the rule of thumb "when in doubt, do nothing" were probably decisive for many. And for many who did vote, the corollary was: don't try anything new for the *first* time. The opposition vote was more than half in Cuyahoga, almost half in Dade, two-thirds in St. Louis City, and a thumping three-fourths in St. Louis County. Such a vote does not reflect the direct effectiveness of the opposition; instead, it probably reflects the power of basically conservative norms among the voters. They were not involved enough to understand the Plan, and they did not want to vote for something they did not understand.

The politician's response to such a movement is curious and varies greatly. One ward politico in Cleveland worked very hard and almost swung his (traditionally hostile) ward to the new charter. To do so, he "made the Eagle scream,"—citing 1776, home rule, freedom, and democratic rights. Even in St. Louis there is evidence that ward leaders were effective, both pro and con.[4] Most political pros, however, waited until they sensed the direction of opinion in their wards to take a stand on the issue .When they discovered a violent move in one direction or the other, they decided; if (as was usual in St. Louis) they found widespread disinterest, they felt free to take any position they wished. An issue nobody cares about is a vacation from politics, especially if the party hierarchy is also indifferent.

The civic leaders—businessmen, university chancellors, heads of chambers of commerce, and the like—were basically favorable to all

[3] Lang and Lang, *op. cit.*, page 231.
[4] Cf. *Reform in St. Louis*, *op. cit.*, Chapter 5, "The Vote."

three plans. However, their ineptness and impuissance could not be better illustrated than through the story of these campaigns. The debacle of the Negro negotiations in Cleveland indicates the first; the flight of capital from the District Plan in St. Louis, the second. Wherever politics is organized, the "power structure" *must* rely upon committing the political professionals in matters of this kind. The civic leaders can neither force compliance nor mount an alternative campaign at the grass roots. By default, their campaign will be a mass media exercise. And here they will run into the incompetence of voters as judges, the conservatism of the electorate. (Furthermore, the real commitment of business leaders may be questioned. It is likely that, for them, the campaign does not compare in importance with serious matters—that is, business.)

Yet the campaign in Dade County, run by civic leaders, did succeed. The Cuyahoga County Charter came very close. How did this happen? In the absence of really adequate data we can only speculate. We will list some predispositions which seemed to have been favorable to change in these three areas, and some unfavorable. The two in combination were, perhaps, adequate to produce the varying results.

Some Gross Variables

We shall discuss two aspects of the efforts in these three metropolitan areas: First, the nature of the change proposed, for it does seem to have had an effect on the outcome; second, the nature of the campaign.

In St. Louis the District Plan would have created a completely new, unprecedented, and unknown governmental power, the metropolitan district. It would not have abolished any existing government or office and it promised a tax increase rather than tax savings. Further, the campaign for the plan existed in a cultural vacuum—there had been no effort at overall, multifunctional, metropolitan area government since the early 1930's.[5]

[5] There had been defeats of new charters for the City of St. Louis in 1950 and 1957. These, however, had no "metro" implications. Referenda for special district governments, the transit district and the sewer district, emphasized the *specific services*, not the metropolitan areas' general government.

In both Cuyahoga County and Dade County the new charter based the metropolitan government on a known entity, shared by city and suburbs alike—the county. In both areas this county was to have more "home rule," or freedom from the straitjacket of the state constitution. In both areas there was a recent and "usable" past for the campaign to rest on: in 1950, Cuyahoga barely defeated a new charter, and in 1953, Dade County came within a hair's breadth of merging Miami and the county. In both areas the war cry of "efficiency" was merged with that of "home rule"; many elective offices would be abolished in Cuyahoga, and a large number would disappear in Dade—including the sheriff's office with all its employees.

In the ensuing campaigns, those in St. Louis and Cleveland ran into the unyielding opposition of the central city mayor. In both areas the political parties were split, disaffected, or indifferent. In Dade, however, no political organization or major elective office existed, and no effective opposition was organized. In all three cities the charter had the nominal support of business and the all-out support of the newspapers.

We may summarize these gross variables in tabular form, for simplicity's sake (Table 8–1). Such a grossly simplified description of the three campaigns would seem to indicate why the St. Louis effort was such a failure. Yet if we look more closely, we will see that the *status*

Table 8-1. Gross Variables in the Three Campaigns

	St. Louis	Cuyahoga	Dade
1. Business Support	X	X	X
2. Newspaper Support	X	X	X
3. Use of Existing Government Structure		X	X
4. (A Usable Past): "Home Rule"		X	X
5. (A Usable Past): "Efficiency"		X	X
6. Abolition of Offices		X	X
7. Promise of Tax Savings			X
8. Lack of Party Organization			X
9. Lack of Organized Opposition			X

quo—the existence of party organization and the certainty of opposition—forced many other decisions. The constitutional inheritance of a separate county government for the suburbs and central city forced a new device; the time lapse since the last failure was not remediable; the failure to abolish governments and offices rested on a (realistic) estimate of opposition and its base; this in turn prohibited free promises of tax reduction. In Cuyahoga County similar concerns were operative. However, it is obvious that the outcome could have gone either way in Dade and in Cuyahoga: perhaps "higher taxes" is effective only when there is no massive counter-cry such as "Home Rule for Cuyahoga County."

Political Reform and the Voters

From these studies it is clear that transmitting to the electorate the complex issues of structural change in government is a thankless and near-impossible task. The campaign that succeeded was described by its architects as one of "brainwashing" the voters—promising them pie in the sky while ignoring or blacking out opposition voices. For, if they are heard, even five men of stature can greatly complicate an issue.

When the structure of government is to be decided by a public opinion poll (and this is what a referendum turns out to be) the outlook for adjustment of government to other changes going on in the society would appear bleak. The change cannot move far beyond the understanding and normative commitment of the median in the distribution of voters. That, in turn, would seem to be a basically conservative, anti-government position. The alternatives are (1) to manipulate the electorate through redefining (or misdefining) the issue or (2) to bring about change through *fiat*. The former course was taken in Dade County, the latter in Toronto (where the provincial legislature created the metropolitan district government).

These studies have underlined the difficulty of bringing about rational change in a rational manner. However, there are many processes at work indicating that change will take place in the future—whether by rational decisions in referenda, by brainwashing and blackout, by administrative fiat, or by shifts of power to higher levels—to the government of the state or the federal union itself. Such changes will necessarily be partly adventitious; there will be the usual cries of politics and pelf; the results will not satisfy the criteria of rational planners of governments.

Yet such variety is defensible. As long as our knowledge of political life is made up of lore, rule of thumb, and primitive science, it is good to have a variety of experiments going on. The process of political innovation is built into the constitutional-legal framework and has support in the political culture of the American citizenry. Anyone who can raise the money to get enough petitions signed in St. Louis City and County can force the selection of a Board of Freeholders, the drafting of a charter, and a vote on it.

The machinery of government tends, then, to invite continually the attention of the amateurs, or "lovers," of government—the men of good will, the technical innovators, the politicians on the make, the politicians transmitted into statesmen, the chorus of old men. Their efforts to redesign the polity, to move our political life towards another plane more desirable to them, are largely failures. They must survive the attack of that which exists. Their sponsors grow tired, but new generations come on. These efforts to make the Heavenly City may be compared to fish eggs, spawned by the million, lost and devoured by other organisms, but occasionally producing a new model, which could not have been predicted or designed but may have virtues of its own.

Index

Tables